Deeply Defined

ADVANCE PRAISE

"*Deeply Defined* helps us do exactly that—be defined by deep layers of Godly principles. Even for someone like me who is 'seasoned' in the faith, it was good to verify that I was still on the right path in my thinking and choices. Janey's poignant questions lead us all to a vital exploration of the health of our faith. It's easy to forget key truths in the chaos and pressures of our world's dilemmas. So, whether you're in search of what to believe or you too are seasoned in your faith, *Deeply Defined* was written for you."
   —**Patsy Clairmont**, Speaker, Author, Podcaster, Wife, Mom, Nana

"God never changes, but our words about God do. Some new believers come to church without ever knowing its lingo. Others are deeply ingrained in the language of Zion. In *Deeply Defined*, Janey Pitts advocates keeping the meaning while baptizing theological words like justification, sanctification, propitiation, and glorification in contemporary relevance. Her book seeks to equip new believers and those who will witness to the lost with language to comprehend the truth of Scripture in fresh new ways."
   —**Dr. Robert Smith, Jr.**, Charles T. Carter Baptist Chair of Divinity,
Beeson Divinity School, Samford University

"Janey's seminary training allows her to take a deep dive into the Scriptures. Her experiences as a wife, mother, and friend enable her to draw practical applications to truth."
   —**Eva Whittington Self**, Women's Speaker,
Author, *May Bell's Daughter*

"*Deeply Defined* is a refreshing contribution to Christian literature. Janey's writing style is conversational but make no mistake about it; she takes her readers deep into Hebrew and Greek word studies, leading one to say, 'Ahh, now, I get it.' Janey's illustrations are lively, relevant, and serve to illuminate the main points. *Deeply Defined* takes its readers beyond superficial Bible studies by employing exegetical skills in a way that truly exposes key Bible passages but doesn't lose its readers in academic jargon, so get ready for a deep dive into God's Word! When you turn the last page of *Deeply Defined*, you will feel as if you are good friends with Janey Pitts, and more importantly, you will grow in your understanding of God's Word. I heartily recommend this book."

—**Ray Rhodes, Jr.**, Author, *Yours, till Heaven:*
The Untold Love Story of Charles and Susie Spurgeon
and *Susie: The Life and Legacy of Susannah Spurgeon*

"How does our faith in Christ shape us, and what do words like grace, mercy, and hope, mean? These are questions that are answered in *Deeply Defined* as we learn to become more like him, shaped by his love and mercy rather than our own insecurities. I can't imagine a more timely book for this generation who needs to know not only who God is, but how we are defined by him."

—**Lance Howerton**, President, Crossings Ministries

"Janey's writing holds deep reverence of Scripture and carries stories that bring a sense of awe and hope. This book brings Truth to life through stories, wisdom, and context. You will grow closer to God and be developed as your curiosity is sparked by the questions at the end of the chapters!"

—**Sandhya Oaks**, TEDx Speaker, Ministry Leader

DEEPLY DEFINED
Understanding Who You Are In Christ

JANEY PITTS

NASHVILLE

NEW YORK • LONDON • MELBOURNE • VANCOUVER

Deeply Defined
Understanding Who You are in Christ

Published in New York, New York, by Morgan James Publishing. Morgan James is a trademark of Morgan James, LLC. www.MorganJamesPublishing.com

Proudly distributed by Ingram Publisher Services.

Morgan James BOGO™

A **FREE** ebook edition is available for you or a friend with the purchase of this print book.

CLEARLY SIGN YOUR NAME ABOVE

Instructions to claim your free ebook edition:
1. Visit MorganJamesBOGO.com
2. Sign your name CLEARLY in the space above
3. Complete the form and submit a photo of this entire page
4. You or your friend can download the ebook to your preferred device

ISBN 9781631956119 paperback
ISBN 9781631956126 ebook
Library of Congress Control Number:
2021937216

Cover Design by:
Megan Dillon
megan@creativeninjadesigns.com

Interior Design by:
Christopher Kirk
www.GFSstudio.com

Morgan James is a proud partner of Habitat for Humanity Peninsula and Greater Williamsburg. Partners in building since 2006.

Get involved today! Visit MorganJamesPublishing.com/giving-back

For Mom, Dad, Cory, Charlie, and Elizabeth

TABLE OF CONTENTS

ACKNOWLEDGMENTS

There are so many people who made this book happen. First, I'd like to thank the Lord for allowing me to write this book; it never would have happened if he hadn't given me the nudge that would not go away until I finished it. My prayer is that this book will deepen others in your word and your ways. It is for, and all about, you.

Karen Anderson, you are amazing. Your energy and wisdom have encouraged me in this process from the very beginning with Morgan James, and I can't tell you how much I appreciate you pouring into me. And to Sissi Haner, I can't imagine a better editor who is kinder and better at their job than you; you are fantastic!

To all the amazing people at Morgan James Publishing—David Hancock, Wes Taylor, Jim Howard, Bonnie Rauch, Taylor Chaffer, and the rest from print to artwork, you guys have been fabulous to work with. Thank you for believing in me and in *Deeply Defined*. It is an honor and joy to be one of your authors!

Danya, it's crazy how thankful I am for you even though we've never met face to face. The information you shared with me was invaluable, and you helped get me on this current trajectory. I will be forever grateful. And Kristi, thanks for the talk and the spicy tuna rolls; both were amazing. I can't wait to see all the ways God is going to use you on a global scale!

I have so many friends to thank who kept me going in the process. To Betsi, for being the first to have eyes on my document. Natalie, Heather, Laura, Amy, and Kathleen, my girls from all over America who took six weeks out of their lives to do a test run as a bible study and give me feedback each week—I love you all. To my Lead Pastor Kevin Lee, who is the best senior pastor I've had the privilege to serve with. Big thanks to my buddy, coach, and cheerleader Dick Savage for his wisdom and joy. My love and thanks to Lindsey and Melissa for the eggs, your excitement, friendship, and for turning mumbo jumbo into words I could understand.

Many thanks to those who let me tell your stories. Thanks to Lowell, who has lived one amazing, God-filled life. To Shannon, who has walked through the fire and is an absolute rock star. To Tray and Melody, who minister to so many bringing hope. To Kinley, who is precious and will never forget how to set a clock. To Jimmy, who truly was transformed. To Abigail, who loves others so well. To Eva, for letting me tell part of your story; you are a light. To Katie, keep using that gift you have to share the gospel; you make it look so easy. *Merci à* Elizabeth, *ma végétarienne préférée.* And thanks to Michael (a homeless man) for reminding me of the power of God.

I have to say thank you to my mom and dad, who brought me up loving the Lord and being wonderful examples of what it means to be a Jesus follower. I love you both, and I'm so proud you are my parents! And Daddy, your advice has gotten me through so much, this book included. You're still the smartest man I know! And to Gee and Papa, who were so excited when I first told you about this and to hear about each step along the way.

Thanks to Charlie and Elizabeth for being the most outstanding offspring on the planet. You have been encouraging, excited with me, and awesome; you guys bring your dad and me so much joy and laughter. I love you both!

And a huge, massive thanks to Cory Pitts. My best friend, soul mate, confidant, and proof "listener" over and over again. You are incredible. Your support has been steady and strong throughout this process, and it means more than you will ever know. I love you so much, and I'd pick you every time!

INTRODUCTION

My husband, Cory, and I are coffee snobs. We didn't aspire to join the caffeinated elite, we just kind of tumbled into it. It all started when we tasted pour-over coffee. If you've never heard of pour-over, it's different from a regular cup of joe. Pour-over is made with freshly ground coffee beans and water from a handheld kettle. I don't know all the science of why it's so shockingly fabulous, but it is a million miles away from anything I'd ever had before. In our house, we have life *before* pour-over coffee and life *after* pour-over coffee.

Soon after it passed our lips, we had a special kettle mailed to our house plus a scale that measures the grounds into grams to enjoy this nectar of the gods at home. We eventually moved from simply grinding our own beans to buying *green* coffee beans and getting a roaster to "up" our game. Before we knew it, we could tell an Ethiopian bean from a Nicaraguan one. We pre-warm the cups with hot water so the coffee stays heated longer while in the mugs. And if that's not enough, a few weeks ago, we switched from tap water to special brew water (not even kidding) so the taste can come through clear and bold and strong. The short of it is when we get into something, man, do we go all out.

That's what happened with our interest in biblical culture. We both are seminary trained and lean toward the nerdy side of things. About ten years ago, we attended a conference explaining the Jewish feasts and how they related to Christ. We realized how studying biblical culture was opening our eyes and hearts to a deeper understanding of Scripture. We were hooked. Shortly after, Cory went back for his doctorate and wrote about the Sabbath. After he graduated, I began what is now this book.

At the time, I wrote a study series for a group in our church called "Defined." I used Greek and Hebrew words, along with biblical culture, to explain terms church people use all the time but can't seem to explain when asked. Grace, mercy, hope, and glory just to name a few. As I kept learning more, I realized how the Bible was opening up to me in a new light. Hebrew idioms and common examples of Jesus's day were helping Scripture come alive in my soul. I wanted everyone to grow closer to Christ the same way I was by reading the Bible through the culture in which it was written.

I entitled this book *Deeply Defined*, and it has a double meaning. First, we are going to use biblical culture and the original languages of the Bible to define words Christians use all the time but can't really explain when pressed. Words like grace, mercy, glory… the list goes on. Second, we are going to learn to apply these biblical concepts to our life and become *Deeply Defined* by understanding who we are to be in the Lord.

This book dives into things headfirst, and just to prepare you, the first several chapters are pretty intense. For us to be Deeply Defined by our Creator, we have to strive to see him in a more intimate way. We begin by examining the holiness of God. It's a deep subject but one we must understand.

Psalm 18:12 states, "God is great, beyond our knowledge." No one will ever fully define God because if we could do that, he would be no different than us. In our limited human capacity, we will not grasp the totality of his being this side of heaven. But we can see a fuller picture of who he is by breaking down the qualities and traits he displays to us every day. And what better way to compare and contrast God's holiness than with our sin?

Those sin chapters keep us in the depths of introspection, but they are important.

It's imperative we look at sin, mull it over, and understand why it's not God's plan for our lives. Those sections examine the underrated topics of confession and repentance and then end with the all-encompassing gift of God's love. We will contemplate the beautiful reality of forgiveness. We will see why our mistakes are not what define us and why it is the Lord who gives us confidence, security, and boldness to live for him.

From there, we will learn to define ourselves by allowing the Spirit of God inside us to carry us along rather than by outside influences. The attitudes of holiness, grace, hope, joy—all of these and more will be explained and then applied to shape and define our lives on a deeper level. We will explore peace and wisdom and all that is associated with them. In the end, you will have a fuller view of what the Scriptures say and who the Scriptures say *you are* in Christ. And in the back of the book, there is a great resource for you to refer to when you need it. It's a list of all the definitions this book covers to help you in your personal Bible study when you need to remember the original meaning of a biblical word.

I am excited to share this book with you, and I think we will become fast friends. So... let's begin our journey together focusing on the Lord! Let's start right now and become *Deeply Defined* by the one who made us.

By His Grace,
Janey

Chapter One

SETTING APART GOD'S HOLINESS

Have you ever tried to describe the taste of meat to a vegetarian? It's impossible.

I, a joyful carnivorous type, was having lunch with an herbivore friend of mine. I had just returned from vacation in Bar Harbor, Maine. If you've never been there, it's a place for your bucket list. The hiking and views in Acadia National Park are exquisite, and the fresh seafood and picturesque town of Bar Harbor are good for the heart and mind. Prior to that trip, I'd never tasted lobster, but I was instantly hooked. Once I returned to my real life, I *had* to tell my friend about it. My desire was to give the best descriptor I could think of, so I started comparing the taste of lobster to butter-slathered shrimp. To a *vegetarian*.

I received a blank stare.

With a grin, I immediately did a mental pivot, possibly adding to my passion that she must understand the greatness of this dish. I did, after all, eat it while wearing a bib. For some reason, I moved to grilled grouper. Now, keep the stare, but add a twinkle and a mouth twitch. To her entertainment, I kept going, but nothing could capture the taste or texture of lobster simply because it was outside any comparable realm she could remember. We ended up in laughter, and because of my lack of proper explanation, she may think lobster tastes like celery. I wanted her to understand, and she wanted to understand, but it just wasn't going to happen.

When we try to define God and his holiness, we wrestle with the same problem. We have a hard time grasping the totality of him because "holy" doesn't describe a disposition. Holiness is woven into the fiber of God's being. Although holy can be used as an accurate description of God, the concept is much deeper than a personality attribute. God's holiness cannot be removed, separated, or ignored from God himself. Holiness is not an emotion that changes and should not be confined to his actions alone. We are called to live a life of holiness, but only God is fully, completely, and thoroughly holy.

All of his goodness, love, grace, forgiveness, mercy, and power stem from holiness. Creation comes from holiness. Salvation comes from holiness. Peace comes from holiness. The fact that God is holy is the foundation for our relationship with him.

The Hebrew word used for holy in the Bible is *qadosh,* and its Greek counterpart is *hagios.* Both include the concept of separateness or distance. If a being or object is holy, it is distinct and different, divided from other things. It literally means to divide, marking off something, setting it apart from something else.[1]

Now that you've read *part* of the Hebrew definition of holiness, read the Psalm 99 passage below. To make this hit home easier, replace the word *holy* with its meaning of *set apart* as you read. Seeing God as separate and set apart from creation will deepen your view of this psalm and your understanding of his holiness.

The Lord reigns, let the nations tremble; he sits enthroned between the cherubim, let the earth shake. Great is the Lord in Zion; he is exalted over all the nations. Let them praise your great and awesome name—he is holy. The King is mighty, he loves justice—you have established equity; in Jacob you have done what is just and right. Exalt the Lord our God and worship at his footstool; he is holy. Moses and Aaron were among his priests, Samuel was among those who called on his name; they called on the Lord and he answered them. He spoke to them from the pillar of cloud; they kept his statutes and the decrees he gave them. Lord our God, you answered them; you were to Israel a forgiving God, though you punished their misdeeds. Exalt the Lord our God and worship at his holy mountain, for the Lord our God is holy.

At the beginning of creation, the Bible introduces us to the main character of the universe. Genesis 1:1–2 says, "In the beginning God created the heavens and the earth. Now the earth was formless and empty, darkness was over the surface of the deep, and the Spirit of God was hovering over the waters."

We immediately see important aspects of God's holiness. God is the Creator, not the created. He has always been and will always be (Revelation 22:13). He exists outside of creation. He is separate, above, and beyond us. He doesn't need us to sustain him or to make him great. God didn't have to create the world; he chose to do so out of his love.

God exists complete and perfect outside of our world. He exists outside of time. The sun, the deciding factor of our days, wasn't even created until day four (Genesis 1:16). He doesn't *need* a relationship with us. He already has a relationship within himself.

John 1:2 states that Jesus, "the Word," existed *with* God in the beginning. We see the Holy Spirit hovering over the waters in Genesis 1:2. When we take a fuller view of what was happening in Genesis, we see the first verse of the Bible introduces us to the Trinity—God, the Father; God, the Son; and God as the Holy Spirit were all present.

He hovered.
He created.
He existed... *before* time.

There is none like our God in the past, present, or future. But the world we live in can be distracting, and God's awesome holiness gets diminished in our minds. Time alone with the Lord gets shoved to the side to fill lunchboxes, prayers get sidetracked with grocery lists, and intimacy with the one who knit us together is crowded out by other people's voices, our worries, or family plans. Without realizing it, the "seen" begins to trump the "unseen."

We then shrink-to-fit our view of the *unlimited* God so it can be explained by our *limited* understanding. We confine the power of the universe to fit what we can grasp in our heads. In our minds, the God of the Universe loses his set-apartness because we focus only on power we can explain or understand, making it seem ordinary. But God is *not* ordinary. As we focus on his holiness, let's bring back the awe, the fear, and reverence of our Creator to our daily routine. In Job 38, God speaks directly to Job. Imagine being on the receiving end of that conversation! In the previous chapters of Job, various people have tried to explain God and his ways. The Lord basically has had enough, steps in, and makes a few points. My knees knock just thinking about that. I'm glad I wasn't around for *that* conversation! The awe, fear, and reverence come pretty easily when we read it as if we were there... In Job 38:4 God asks, "Where were you when I laid the earth's foundation?" In verse 8 God asks, "Who shut up the sea behind doors?" In verse 12 we find God is the one who showed dawn "its place." The point? He is the holy and set-apart Creator, and we are the limited and very much created beings of his handiwork.

God is set apart from his creation. Isaiah 55:8–9 says, "For my thoughts are not your thoughts, neither are your ways my ways," declares the Lord. "As the heavens are higher than the earth, so are my ways higher than your ways and my thoughts than your thoughts."

Can we just stop and appreciate for a moment that his ways are higher than our ways? How great is that? My ways are messy, flawed, insecure, unstable, and many times, second-guessed. But the Lord, the Creator God of the Universe, his ways are perfect, just like him. They are sure, steadfast, and everlasting. Sometimes, we don't understand his ways until we begin to walk in them, and that is when we experience his glory.

Dr. Lowell Gess was a ninety-four-year-old retiree when the Ebola outbreak occurred in Sierra Leone. He had served as a missionary in Africa for fifty-two years of his life, and although he had long been retired, his heart was still with the African people. Most of the foreign doctors left Sierra Leone so as not to become infected with Ebola, and this exodus left very few doctors in the country. The people were hurting and desperate.

Dr. Gess had been praying for Sierra Leone but felt moved to do more. He knew two things. First, being in his mid-nineties, he didn't have much longer on this earth. And second, the people of Sierra Leone needed a doctor. He wanted to go but worried about what his family would think. When he told his loved ones that he had decided to go, they supported his calling; a granddaughter even called it "cool." However, he couldn't go to Sierra Leone without medicine and other supplies.

He rounded up equipment, medicine, and supplies to fill seven fifty-pound boxes, but the airline would only allow him two suitcases. He had no idea how he would get the boxes over, and after much discussion, the airlines agreed to let him take only one box more. So, he started to pray.

He received a phone call from another doctor he had never met who was having a similar problem getting her supplies on a plane. She explained that, while praying about the issue, she had an awareness of two angels being at an airline counter. She prayed for him, then hung up. He decided to quit fighting the airlines and let God do his thing.

His trip was approaching, and even though he had been told he was allowed two suitcases and only one extra box, he took all seven boxes, along with his luggage, to the airport. Upon arrival, the baggage handlers came out, put his luggage and the seven boxes on carts, and whisked them away without blinking an eye. The clerk checked in Dr. Gess, *along with all his boxes and bags*, gave him a ticket, and then wished him a nice flight.

What?!

Nothing was said about the extra bags. No extra money was charged. God had reached through his higher ways into the situation and provided for Dr. Gess and the people of Sierra Leone. The good doctor didn't have to understand how God did it; he just knew God had been faithful.[2] And, in case you were wondering, this July, Dr. Gess will celebrate his one-hundredth birthday.

God's ways *cannot* be measured by our understanding because he is so far ahead of us in knowledge and power. He spoke and life began. Grass and trees sprouted from his lips and birds flew from his thoughts. His breath lit up the galaxy. God is separate, above, and beyond us. He is fullness of wisdom, power, strength, mercy, justice, and forgiveness. His power is limitless, infinite, and immeasurable, outside of anything we can comprehend. We should worship him in awe.

A.W. Tozer said, "To say that God is infinite is to say that He is measureless. Measurement is the way created things have of accounting for themselves. It describes limitations, imperfections, and cannot apply to God… We also try to measure abstract qualities, and speak of great or little faith, high or low intelligence, large or meager talents. It is not plain that all this does not and cannot apply to God? It is the way we see the works of His hands, but not the way we see Him. He is above all this, outside of it, beyond it. Our concepts of measurement embrace mountains and men, atoms and stars, gravity, energy, numbers, speed, but never God. We cannot speak of measure or amount or size or weight and at the same time be speaking of God, for these tell of degrees and there are no degrees in God… Nothing in God is less or more, or large or small. He is what He is in Himself, without qualifying thought or word. He is simply God."[3]

So, we end this chapter with only part of the definition for holiness. God in his holiness is measureless, infinite, above us, and beyond any comprehension. He is set apart. He is deeper, and wider, and wiser, and wonderful. The Creator differs from the created. Psalm 96:9 says, "Worship the Lord in the splendor of his holiness; tremble before him, all the earth!"

Chapter Question

How would you describe God in his holiness?

Chapter Two

THE GLORY OF HIS HOLINESS

ast night the stars were bright, family was close at hand, and the late summer evening temperatures were perfect. We were looking through my daughter's new telescope at the moon, Jupiter, and other cool celestial things. They all were beautiful, but Saturn, with those glorious rings, got me all choked up.

I knew I was in a holy moment. Saturn, being separate from Earth, is above and beyond it. It is over 880 million miles away from us[4], yet I had been given something that allowed me to see its shape and massiveness more clearly. Do you know that 700 Earths would fit inside of Saturn?[5] The God of the Universe made it, and he, in that moment, gave me the gift of enjoying it. I got a glimpse of God's infinite creativity and became acutely aware of the limitations of man. All I could do was worship and stand in awe.

The book of Job describes God's creative power several times, but Job 26:14 ties together the enormity of creation and our Creator in one fantastic sentence. It says, after listing off awesome and creative things only God can do, "And these are but the outer fringe of his works; how faint the whisper we hear of him! Who then can understand the thunder of his power?"

Job is aware he only sees a *hint* of the awesomeness of God in the expansiveness and beauty of creation. If our universe is simply a whisper of God, what is the all-consuming thunder of his power like?

I live roughly twenty miles from an army base. Whenever they have drills involving various types of ammunition, no one can ignore or deny that military training is going on. The ground will shake, and the booms and pops and thunder of the guns echo through the air. We are completely aware that something heavy is being fired and affecting everything around it. And I know we only feel a hint of the impact that a soldier ten feet away from the action experiences.

It is impactful, heavy, even earth-shaking when our limited thoughts contemplate an unlimited God. When I think about a God who is powerful and glorious, and above us and beyond us, it humbles me to my knees. There is reverence, but also fear. There is curiosity and awe. I want to pull close, but yet I am terrified. The power and might that cause *me* trembling and trepidation are but a *whisper* of the Lord. Creation for him was an effortless breath, showing only a glimpse of his holiness. There is grace in the fact that God knows we can't understand the fullness of his glory.

He is Creator, and we are the created.
He *knows* he can't reveal all of who he is to us.
We can't handle it.

You know, Job isn't the only Bible character who has trembled at the glorious power of God. Maybe you have trembled in your life at his power too. The Bible is full of illustrations, but here are some to get us going.

Moses quivered at the burning bush.
Daniel fainted after seeing God's vision of the future.
Paul shook on the road to Damascus.

What is it they understood or experienced when they were face to face with something greater than themselves? The following two verses may give us a clue. As you read them, note the two common words that we are to ascribe to the Lord.

Psalm 29:1–2 says, "Ascribe to the Lord, you heavenly beings, ascribe to the Lord glory and strength. Ascribe to the Lord the glory due his name; worship the Lord in the splendor of his holiness."

In 1 Chronicles 16:28–29 it says, "Ascribe to the Lord, all you families of nations, ascribe to the Lord glory and strength. Ascribe to the Lord the glory due his name; bring an offering and come before him. Worship the Lord in the splendor of his holiness."

Glory and strength popped out, didn't they?

The Hebrew word for *glory* has an interesting etymology (a fancy word for saying where a word came from) from early in biblical times. Unpacking this word and understanding the culture in which the bible was written is going to help us see the Scriptures on a deeper level. Instead of just telling you the meaning, I want you to see it so you can freak out about it as much as I did. Because as we say in the South, it is *cool as grits*. Look at the following verses and note the words that are equated with glory.

"But you, Lord, are a shield around me, my glory, the One who lifts my head high" (Psalm 3:3).

"My glory will not fade; the bow will be ever new in my hand"
(Job 29:20).

In the above verses, glory is compared to a shield and a bow. The Hebrew word *kavod* (glory) gets its meaning from battle armaments! The literal meaning of glory means heavy, or weighty, like a sword or shield or bow would be if you were holding them. Because of this, the word glory also has taken on a meaning of importance and honor.[6]

When we read about the glory of the Lord, we need to grasp his weighty presence and power. There are all kinds of emotionally charged biblical examples where it states the glory of the Lord was *seen*. Jesus told Martha she would see the glory of God right before Lazarus came out of the grave (John 11:40). In Exodus, God's glory appeared to his people in the cloud (Exodus 16:10). Stephen saw the glory of God as he was being stoned (Acts 7:55). When the angels appeared to the shepherds, the glory of the Lord shone about them (Luke 2:9). Jesus is described as the radiance of God's glory (Hebrews 1:3), and Isaiah prophesied that through Christ, the glory of God would be revealed (Isaiah 40:5). In all of these situations, the glory—the weighty, important holiness of our Creator—is physically seen and experienced.

God's glory is revealed to us when, *in his holiness*, he interacts with man.

You may have heard the term *shekinah glory* used at some point. I always thought it had something to do with a bright light, and maybe a glow-y person or something. I was wrong on both counts! That word was coined by Jewish rabbis to describe a part of God's character. It literally means "that which dwells" and is first seen in God's Word when the Israelites had escaped from Egypt. God was with them in the cloud and pillar of fire, day and night. He dwelt with them. His cloud provided shade in the sweltering desert heat as he guided them and a guiding light at night as he watched over them.

They could *see* the Lord's presence around them.
They could *feel* the coolness or warmth as he watched over them.
They could *hear* when the sea was blown back to make dry ground.

The term shekinah glory is a powerful way of stating the presence of the Lord was seen and felt and *experienced* by the people.[7]

There is weight and importance in our glorious Holy God, and we understand it best when we ask him to dwell in our hearts. When we accept Jesus and invite the Spirit of God into our lives, our relationship becomes acutely personal. We no longer are dealing with a distant God we've heard about but an up-close, personal deity who desires to be intimately involved in our lives. Stop for a moment and think about God's glory. When was the last time you experienced the Lord's presence in a deep, personal way?

This winter we had a pretty big snowfall. Our basement has French doors that offer a beautiful view of our backyard, which is abundant with large, old trees. I was snuggled under a blanket in a huge comfy chair, the lights were low, and I had a cup of my favorite tea in hand.

As I watched the thick, penny-sized snowflakes fall to the ground, I was overwhelmed with thankfulness for my life. A happy and healthy family, amazing friends, a warm home, a church and staff that I adore, and a God of the Universe who knows my name. All I could do was worship. I was completely overwhelmed by all the Lord has done for me, a sinner, saved by his grace. When I call to him, he answers. He surrounds me with his love, wisdom, and mercy. It was an ordinary moment that he entered into and made it holy. It was wonderful.

In Scripture, we see God doing this with other people too. Psalm 24 is a beautiful picture of the King of the Universe entering into his rightful place. David, the author of this psalm, takes us on the journey with our Lord. The journey starts with creation and moves to the ascending hill of the Lord. The doors open so the King of Glory can enter his tabernacle.

Charles Spurgeon tells us David wrote this psalm to be sung when the ark of the Lord was being taken from Obed-Edom's home into Jerusalem.[8] I want you to see verses seven through ten of Psalm 24 (NASB) now that you know the cultural meaning of glory:

> Lift up your heads, O gates, and be lifted up, O ancient doors, that the King of Glory may come in! Who is this King of Glory? The Lord strong and mighty, the Lord mighty in battle. Lift up your heads, O gates, and life them up, O ancient doors, that the King of Glory may come in! Who is this King of Glory? The Lord of Hosts, he is the King of Glory.

David knew from experience the Lord was mighty in battle. He had fought for David and the Israelites again and again. Now that we are aware that the word glory came from a battlefield, we can better understand that God fights for us too. Our glorious God is a personal God who is to be experienced and included in our lives every day.

God's glory is to be experienced, just as is his holiness. Isn't it wonderful he doesn't keep his glory to himself, and his holiness extends beyond the meaning of being set apart! His glory, like those army drills, cannot be hidden. It is heavy, weighty, and important. God's holiness is woven into the fabric of his being, and it is too vast, too awesome, and too *glorious* to ignore.

Chapter Question

When have you experienced the glory of God on a personal level?

Chapter Three

HOLY, HOLY, HOLY

The prophet Isaiah also witnessed our glorious and holy God when he experienced a vision of God in the temple. We have already covered that God in his holiness is separate, above, and beyond. We have covered that his holiness is weighty, important, and heavy. Now we will move even deeper into understanding why God chooses to reach down and interact with his creation.

This is a heavy-but-important one folks, so if you need to, grab a beverage, snuggle up in a blanket, and settle in. If I could, I'd promise you some snow outside your window, but that's not up to me. Plus, you might be reading this on the beach in July. So, to use beach terminology, today is the deepest water we are going to be in when it comes to the concept of holiness. Let's dive in so we can understand more about the Lord!

Isaiah 6:1–7 is a passage that is probably familiar to you. It's talking about Isaiah's call and mission from the Lord. To give us a time reference, this passage starts out with a little name-dropping. King Uzziah had reigned for fifty-two years but had just passed away. He had been a good king and was the only king over Judah to this point in Isaiah's lifetime.

15

Notice that Isaiah mentions a dead earthly king to provide a time reference, while in the same breath brings awe when describing the infinite King of the Universe. Immediately we see hope. Immediately we see a power greater than Uzziah. King Uzziah could sit on a throne, but only the King of the Universe could fill the temple with his splendor and might. And that is what he goes on to describe.

Isaiah 6:3 tells us that seraphim stand above the throne of God and call out, "Holy, holy, holy is the Lord Almighty; the whole earth is full of his glory."

This repetition of words is found only one other time in the Bible (Revelation 4:8) and again is by heavenly creatures praising God's holiness. To understand this form of repeated praise used in biblical culture, let's go back to our high school grammar class.

In English, we use comparatives or superlatives as word extensions, such as *happy, happier, happiest*. We rank how strong things are just by altering the last part of the word. But in ancient biblical culture, importance is stressed by repeating the same word over and over. The more the word is repeated, the bigger the deal.

If a word is repeated twice in the Bible, the speaker is trying to get our attention. For instance, Jesus said, "Truly, truly I say unto you…" Since it was repeated twice, it's like Jesus is saying, "Listen up, people, this is super important stuff!" Or we can look at another example that is far more interesting but a lot less known because we can't see it in the English translations of our bible.

Genesis 14 describes when the kings of Sodom and Gomorrah fall into some tar pits. To help the reader understand that these are no ordinary-sized tar pits, the Hebrew doubles down and says these specific pits are the *beeroth, beeroth* or pits, pits. In other words, these tar pits were so huge that there may have been pits inside of the pits. It's a way the writer lets the reader know these pits were massive and far from the norm.

R. C. Sproul states, "Only once in sacred Scripture is an attribute of God elevated to the third degree. Only once is a characteristic of God mentioned three times in succession. The Bible says God is holy, holy, holy. Not that He is merely holy, or even holy, holy. He is holy, holy, holy. The Bible never says God is love, love, love; or mercy, mercy, mercy; or wrath, wrath, wrath; or justice, justice, justice. It does say that He is holy, holy, holy, that the whole earth is full of His glory."[9]

We find Isaiah in the throne room of Heaven,
   gazing at beings he has never seen,
     who are proclaiming the highest praise possible,
    to the Most Holy God.

And, if being in a room with The Great I Am wasn't overwhelming enough, there was more going on than sights and sounds. According to Isaiah 6:4, the foundations of the doorways started shaking at the sound of their voices, and the temple filled with smoke. It was more intense than a 4D ride at a theme park! The very words they were saying in praise overwhelmed creation, and the room itself was responding.

This was a full body worship experience. Sometimes I wonder if doorposts and thresholds understand the presence of the Lord better than we do. They quake in his presence, and so many times we don't even take the time to enter it. Isaiah, however, was keenly aware he was in the presence of God's pure and glorious set-apartness. He was so overwhelmed and affected that he declared "Woe to me... I am a man of unclean lips... I live among a people of unclean lips!"

This is a huge deal because it is the only time in Scripture a prophet proclaims "woe" (judgment) on himself. As Isaiah stands in the presence of complete holiness, he is faced with the crushing weight of his own sin and the sinfulness of all humanity.

Dwight Pryor says it so well: "We tend to just disregard the whole issue of the holiness of God. The world at large has humanized God and deified man to such an extent that there is no longer any distinction between the two, no distinction between the holy and the profane. But we, the people of God (I believe) need to be and shall be restored to a fuller understanding that our God is a holy God, and in that restoration there will be transformation."[10]

How do we humanize God? We start thinking if we believe something, he must see things from our perspective too. Or worse, we begin to believe we know better than God.

It reminds me of a t-shirt I saw while in seminary. On it was a quote from Friedrich Nietzsche. Ol' Freddy was a German philosopher who wrote a lot on the concepts of good and evil. He was incredibly intelligent, but unfortunately, lost his mind in his older years. His big thing was that we could all become a "super-man" if we could just "kill God."

Yes, you read that right.

So, this t-shirt had two quotes on it. The first was a quote from Nietzsche, who happened to pass away in the year 1900. It said, in very small letters,

"God is dead."
—Nietzsche

It was quoting him on one of the things he taught and believed. Then, under it, in quite a large font was another sentence that read,

"Nietzsche is dead."
—God

God always gets the last word my friend, whether we believe that or not. Our eternal God knows best because he is above and beyond us. He is weighty and important and honorable. He is earth-forming, earth-flooding, and earth-finishing. We must never, ever forget that he is God and we are not.

When we humanize God and deify man, we lose sight of God's holy perfection and purity. We become immune to sin around us and accept it as a normal way of life. We explain sin away because it makes us feel better, and we begin to compare ourselves to others and their standards rather than the Lord. If we compare our sin to other sinners, we have removed perfection as a benchmark and have put ourselves on some sadistic sliding scale that ranges from pity to pride.

God doesn't want us to be bound by the weight, burden, or guilt of sin. When we stare into the ugly face of our iniquity, we become aware of our need for a savior. Facing perfection shows the depth of our need. If the evil one can make us forget God's holiness, our sin can be diminished in our eyes, which means we become less aware of our raw, utter need for God to rescue us.

Isaiah was staring at the face of pure, glorious holiness. He literally was beholding perfection, which enlightened him to the darkness of his shortcomings and sin. But God didn't desire for Isaiah to stay fearful, depressed, and forlorn that he was a sinful man. God didn't shame Isaiah in his sin or ban him from his presence. God offered hope. A relationship. Forgiveness. Isaiah 6:6–7 tells us that one of the seraphim flew with a hot coal and touched Isaiah's mouth. He then explained to Isaiah that his sin was removed.

Our God is a restorative and loving God. Because he exists in a realm outside of the one he created, he reaches into our reality to interact with his people. Here, God meets Isaiah and cleanses him from his sin with an angel and a burning coal.

That's a scary thought, isn't it? The action was symbolic; remember, this was a vision.

Fire in Scripture almost always refines, purifies, and cleanses. The experience of a coal touching Isaiah's lips seems terrifying, but Isaiah is relieved and encouraged by God moving toward him and cleansing him from his sin. God reaches into our lives too, and just because God's interaction with us isn't as dramatic as Isaiah's vision, it doesn't make it any less holy.

Isaiah 57:15 shows that God dwells in a high and holy place but also with the contrite and lowly in spirit. He chooses to reach down from his perfect throne to interact with us, his people.

The Hebrew word for contrite used here is *dakka*, and it means "crushed" or "pulverized like powder." When we have a contrite heart, our spirit is reduced to dust when we contemplate our sin. Our hearts are metaphorically crushed. But with humility comes change. A contrite heart partners with humility, bringing a constant reliance on God. We realize we are nothing without our Creator or his purpose for our lives. But please don't confuse this with thinking you are worthless, as nothing could be further from the truth. Don't second guess our Father, who sacrificed his son because he wants to be with you so badly.

Our sin is worthless, not our soul.

Isaiah was humble with a contrite heart and found himself in the presence of God. The Lord then cleansed Isaiah from his sins. Immediately in the story, God asked whom he could use for his purposes. Immediately Isaiah responded. The first word God said to him was *go*.

When God purifies us from sin and gives us a holy heart, he gives us the positive command to "go." *Go* and love others. *Go* and tell about me. *Go* and be an extension of my love to other people.

First Peter 2:9 says, "But you are a chosen people, a royal *priesthood,* a holy nation, God's special possession, that you may declare the praises of him who called you out of darkness into his wonderful light."

Martin Luther taught that all Christians should act like priests, even if a person was just a simple milkmaid or plowman.[11] Since I was raised Protestant, the whole priest idea didn't really register with me. I knew I could go directly to the Father and ask him for anything because of Jesus's redemptive work on the cross. But when I understood the ancient culture of the Bible, I see it means so much more.

If you're not careful, your eyes may glaze over while reading the last few chapters of Exodus. I know mine can! Before I even realize it, I'm scanning all the lists, not really taking anything into my brain or my heart. Exodus uses the last few chapters to check off how many pounds of things were given to the tabernacle. It lists lengths and widths and breadths and bronzes and golds and silvers and yarns and things I wonder how in the world relate to me. But Exodus 39 *does* relate to me. And it relates to you too. Exodus 39 describes the priestly garments. And no, this is not a fashion guide. It does, however, have some interesting things we can apply to our lives.

The Bible describes the top part of the priestly garment, the ephod. The ephod was the sleeveless garment that went over a white linen robe. Two stones engraved with six names each of the twelve tribes of Israel were sewn into the shoulders of the garment. This means Aaron, the high priest, literally felt the weight of the tribes of Israel on his shoulders whenever he wore it.

There was also an embroidered breastplate that held twelve stones set in gold, each engraved with a name of a tribe of Israel. Again, the high priest would literally feel the weight of God's people over his heart. On the bottom of a blue robe—that went over the white linen but under the ephod—there were gold bells and blue, purple, and scarlet yarn pomegranates. As the high priest walked, he even sounded different than a normal person because the bells would jingle. Finally, he would don a turban that held a medallion that said, "Holy to the Lord."

From head to toe, the high priest, when he dressed, would be reminded that he was called to be holy. He shouldered the weight of the people. His heart was heavy because of the people. And since we are all priests in the eyes of the Lord, we should bear the weight of others on our shoulders. Pray for the hurting, help the lost, feed the hungry. We should reach in and interact with others as we live out the greatest command of loving God and loving our fellow man.

We are to be holy as he is holy. God in his holiness interacts with his people. God is *separate, above, and beyond us, but chooses to reach into our world and interact with us.* That is holiness. That is how God interacts with us. That is a God who seeks out a deep and meaningful relationship with his creation.

Chapter Question

Knowing the full definition of holiness, how are we to be holy as we interact with those around us?

Chapter Four

PUZZLING HOLINESS

When my kids were small, we loved to work puzzles. We'd pop some corn, fill the sippy cups, and build a fort out of blankets to have a great place to work. We then would spread out the pieces, making sure each one had the bright colors facing up. These puzzles were the simple wooden ones, made for a toddler's hands. Sometimes getting started was easy. Other times, my kids would need assistance. And, as any parent would, I would help.

I could see immediately the piece they needed. I was beyond where they were in their understanding of things such as these. The puzzles were so simple that not only did I know the proper place for the piece in question, but I also could easily see by the outlines in the base where each piece had a home.

My children needed to figure out which piece belonged. They would look and ponder and try out a few that didn't quite fit. When the time was right, when they needed me, I would reach in and help. I might point to the piece. Or "accidentally" knock it to get their attention. Other times I would pick it up and hand it to them with a loving smile.

I communicated with them on their level. Sometimes it was subtle, other times it was obvious.

As an adult, I was both above and beyond them in knowledge and their toddler tactile facilities, but I chose to interact with them out of love. This, my friends, is a parallel of how God, in his holiness, interacts with us.

God's holiness is powerful enough to create a universe yet gentle enough to reveal only what we can handle about his awesomeness. God doesn't *need* a relationship with us, but out of love, he desires to reach down and interact with us on an intimate, personal level. Our God has never been content to sit in separateness when it comes to his people. From the beginning of time, we see him interacting and drawing his people close.

He walked with Adam and Eve in the Garden.
He dined with Moses and seventy elders on top of Mount Sinai.
He spoke to Samuel.
Abraham was his friend.

He sent his son, Jesus, to show us how to live, to die on a cross for our sins. Jesus beat sin and death and rose again. When we believe in him, we can live with him forever.

To continue the thought of "Be holy because I am holy," let's look to Leviticus. In chapter 19:1–2, we find God talking to his chosen people after he delivered them from Egypt. This entire chapter is telling them how to live. He is leading them to act in new ways—they are no longer slaves, but free. In verse one, we see God talking to Moses, and he tells Moses to relay the following message to "the entire assembly of Israel."

Note this message is not just to the men, or the adults, or the nice ones, or just the milkmaids. This message is important enough that it needs to permeate the entire culture. What is the message Moses is to share with anyone who has a heartbeat?

Be holy because I, the Lord your God, am holy.

This is a *corporate statement*, which means it is for all of God's people to do *in unity*. The fact that it is a command removes the option of *not* being holy. This idea of holiness is the basis for all law in Israel. Striving for holiness is the key to worship and obedience in everyday life. Although it is a corporate command, each Christian should emulate God in his or her life. God doesn't expect perfection—Romans 3:10 says, "There is no one righteous, not even one"—but he does expect obedience.

When we have other Christians around us who are striving for the same goals of holiness, we spur one another on. In cycling, racers can go faster and cover more distance easier when they help each other block the wind by drafting each other. It's one reason they have teams, to help one another along and lower the resistance of the wind.

A W Tozer uses a different analogy for corporate holiness: "Has it ever occurred to you that one hundred pianos all tuned to the same fork are automatically tuned to each other? They are of one accord by being tuned, not to each other, but to another standard to which each one must individually bow. So, one hundred worshipers met together, each one looking away to Christ, are in heart nearer to each other than they could possibly be were they to become 'unity' conscious and turn their eyes away from God to strive for closer fellowship."[12]

Striving for holiness as a people of God draws us closer to him and other believers. This creates accountability, a group of one mind to encourage one another and a group that can serve together in unity.

When my kids were younger, I had a group of women friends whose kids were around the same ages as mine. We would meet in a park a few days each week to let the kids play and to give us a chance at real conversation. Those simple playdates turned into a huge blessing in my life because all of these women were God-honoring believers. We would pray together, discuss Scripture, and encourage one another in the Lord. We would laugh, cry, and always lift each other up, never tear anyone down. These ladies encouraged me to grow deeper in my faith, to strive to live a life that was pleasing and holy to the Lord.

Our actions can be holy, but only God *is* holy. It is he who defines us. We need to be constantly aware of our need for him, or we will easily slip into defining ourselves through earthly, temporal, tangible eyes.

There are good and bad things in life that can define us if we aren't careful. Good things like our families, our work, or personal achievements can make us feel good, even confident. And our mistakes, failures, and sins can leave us feeling insecure and ashamed. Good and bad choices, attitudes, and circumstances may define us socially, but they should not define our soul. Only the Lord, Creator of heaven and earth, should define the core of who you are.

We are children of the unlimited, all-powerful God who is holy beyond comprehension. He created you for a reason and a purpose. He has given your life meaning. His desire is to reach down and interact with you every day, defining you in his freedom, grace, mercy, forgiveness, and love. He wants to help you with the puzzle pieces of your life, putting together things that should be together, and keeping separate things that can contaminate your life.

God is your father.
He wants what is best for you.

Second Corinthians 7:1 says, "Therefore, since we have these promises, dear friends, let us purify ourselves from everything that contaminates body and spirit, perfecting holiness out of reverence for God."

This is where our striving for personal holiness hits resistance because the contaminating factor of holiness is sin.

The overarching word for sin in Hebrew is *hhatah* and is the picture of an archer aiming at a target, shooting, and *missing the mark*. Judges 20:16 (NLT) uses the word we translate as sin when it says the archers could hit a target... *without missing*. Sin is an action done in error, a failure.[13]

In 2010, there was a reality show called *Top Shot*. It started with a large group of people who were whittled down to one winner and included marksmen of every kind. Three men were left in the finale— Chris Reed, George Reinas, and "Gunny" Zins. These men had become friends over the course of the show and genuinely cared about one another. Chris and Gunny were middle-aged and had families. George, single and in his mid-twenties, was an army sniper. The challenge at hand was long range, perfect for a highly trained soldier such as George but challenging for Chris and Gunny, who excelled in other areas of marksmanship. George set up for his turn, and all the men watching *knew* this was George's time to shine.

But he didn't.
George missed the mark.

Silent shock wafted over the airwaves. That botched shot meant he'd lost and was going home. No glory, no money, no title. But when asked about missing that shot, George was illusive. The viewer could get the distinct impression that out of his love and respect for Chris, who ended up winning that season, George missed his mark *intentionally*.

Sometimes in life we "miss the mark" because we make a mistake. Other times we "miss the mark" on purpose... except, distinctive from George, we have a darker motive in mind.

Unlike George, our "misses" aren't valiant. Our missing the mark, whether planned or unplanned, is sin. Can you think of a time when you had an unplanned sin pop up out of nowhere? This could be with words, thoughts, or actions. Now think of a time when you knew you were acting wrongly, yet you did it anyway. These sins should hurt your heart. I know mine do.

Our desires must not trump what God desires for us. His will and his ways should always be first and foremost in our lives. When we fall into planned and unplanned sins, we are missing the mark of holiness. We are falling short of the life God intended for us. How can we be separate from sin when we are wallowing in it?

Right now, ask God to help you overcome temptation, whether the sin is planned or not. Let's strive to live out what we have been commanded to do and live in holiness by yielding to our Creator's will in our lives. Allow God victory over those parts of your life, invite him to reach in to interact with you. He will indeed help you out of the hot messes of your life; you just have to ask!

Chapter Question

What is the difference between the shortcomings of sin and the higher ways of holiness?

Chapter Five

NO PAIN, NO GAIN

Congenital insensitivity to pain is a rare disease in which a person is unable to feel any type of physical suffering. At first, this sounds great. To live a life free of migraines and sore muscles? Sign me up! But pain exists to keep us safe. If we are burned, cut, cramping, or writhing, we are aware something is wrong. The pain causes us to get away from the source of whatever is hurting us and seek medical attention when required.

Today's tolerant society doesn't want anyone to feel emotional pain in the form of guilt or shame. At face value, this seems Christlike. But both guilt and shame caused by *our* actions (not actions done *to* us—that, my friend, is not what we are discussing) occur when we have done something wrong. Guilt and shame are painful. And pain is a consequence of sin, whether it is eventual or immediate. Without the weight of consequence, it's easy to ignore or deny any wrongdoing.

A perfect way evil can devour us, is to convince us that our sin is not bad, or wrong, or hurting anyone.

If we believe that, we don't feel the prick of our actions.

When right and wrong are based on opinion, biblical truth becomes obsolete. People define sin depending on their personal agenda or emotion, making truth relative to its owner. This places godliness on a sliding scale, forming a comparative morality that makes us feel pretty good about ourselves. Anything can be justified when we "miss the mark"...

- I'm only speeding so I won't be late for church.
- It was just a little white lie.
- I wasn't gossiping because what I said was true.
- That word popped out. I couldn't help it.
- It's just a bad habit.

Other times we refuse to admit Christlikeness is something we should aim for in the first place, and we begin to become entrapped in a lifestyle of denied sin...

- What's true for one person isn't true for everyone.
- The heart wants what the heart wants.

Oh, friend, sin is real. We need to accept, understand, and admit we are all sinners in need of a savior. Just because something makes us happy does not mean it makes us holy. If we can justify away sin in our lives, Jesus's sacrifice becomes null and void. Why? If there is no sin, there is no need for a savior. So, join me and let's get uncomfortable as we shine the light of Jesus into the darker parts of our lives.

Psalm 32:5 reads, "Then I acknowledged my sin to you and did not cover up my iniquity. I said, 'I will confess my transgressions to the Lord.' And you forgave the guilt of my sin."

The first thing David admits in this psalm is his sin. It's difficult to admit we are wrong, isn't it? An attitude of humility is required, and unfortunately, our culture today seems to see humility as a weakness, which is ridiculous when you think about it. It requires a much deeper character to humbly admit a wrong than it does to ignore and gloss over something. Admitting a wrong is the first step in the process of restoration with someone. If we can't admit something we did was wrong, are we really owning our mistake?

The process of forgiveness and healing begins only when we acknowledge sin is present. When we ignore it and/or are hardened by it, we drift in our faith. God is waiting to forgive, but knows true repentance starts with a broken heart admitting the wrong. If you can, stop and say the words "I am a sinner" out loud right now.

Did you notice the two synonyms for sin listed in Psalm 32:5 above? *Iniquity* and *transgressions* are common words in the Bible, but we don't use them often in casual conversation. But when we look deeper into their definitions, and the cultural references in which they were used, we can begin to grasp the intricacies of sin.

The Hebrew word used for transgressions is *pesha* and means "a revolt, an active rebellion or defiance against an authority." It is willful deviation from the path of righteousness.[14] Transgressions are an *active rebellion or defiance against God.*

When we commit a transgression, our conscience is saying, "*My* will, not *Thy* will." When we transgress, we think we know better than God in what is best for us. Or worse, we don't understand or care what God says and just want what is on the other side of the line. This is why pesha is also translated as trespass. Trespassing is stepping over a boundary line of what God says is right. We usually know when we trespass because we make a choice to go where God says we shouldn't go.

If you are serious about your faith, you *know* when you are in rebellion against God, whether it happens accidentally or on purpose. It can be easy to cross the line from righteousness to wrongness. If we aren't living in an attitude if submission, we can fall into a pit quicker than you can say sin.

Psalm 32:1–2 (CSB) says, "How joyful is the one whose transgression is forgiven, whose sin is covered! How joyful is a person whom the Lord does not charge with iniquity and in whose spirit there is no deceit!" When we run to the Lord and choose to change, there is joy. Every. Single. Time! God is always there to forgive and reinstate us into a relationship with him when we approach him in humility.

In my community, there is a home for women in crisis called Grace and Mercy. It helps women break the cycles of incarceration, addiction, abuse, and homelessness. The program lasts a year and includes housing, Bible studies, education and life skills, counseling, legal assistance, and more. It is fantastic.

The director met Shannon when she visited the jail. Shannon was invited into the year-long program, and she completed it in 2020. Before Grace and Mercy, Shannon had abused drugs and was involved in criminal activity for over twenty years. Her life was dark, hard, and painful. She had been in and out of recovery homes, but because she met Jesus at Grace and Mercy, this time, the Great Physician healed her.

Shannon is now employed as a Peer Support Specialist at the first recovery home she attended. Her youngest son lives with her, and she and her oldest are close as well. Her relationship with her parents has been restored, and they will brag about her to anyone who will listen. Shannon is a strong and dynamic woman who gained the ability to define herself through the eyes of the Lord. God's grace defines her, not her past. Her life verse is Ephesians 5:8 (NLT), which says, "For once you were full of darkness, but now you have light from the Lord. So, live as people of the light!"

What a beautiful picture of restoration and abundant love. That is our God!

If we don't want our lives to get overtaken by sin, correction starts with a humble decision to turn from wrong, walk away, and not go back. The more we wade into the mud pit of sin, the dirtier our souls get and the harder it is to break the cycle. I want us to really understand subtle differences of transgression and iniquity so we can clearly see what we need to walk away from in our lives.

Iniquity (Hebrew *avon*) is sin that differs from transgression by being even more defiant. The cultural reference of the Hebrew word points to crookedness, a moral distortion. Iniquity is not just an action but speaks to the *character* of the action. It is *a premeditated sin that continues in a person's life without remorse or repentance.*[15]

Iniquity in the Bible is on display when Jacob takes Esau's blessing. We see it in David, when he takes Bathsheba as his own, which also sets in motion plans to kill her husband, Uriah. Worst of all, we see iniquity when Judas betrayed Jesus. All of them eventually repented but lived in iniquity for a time. Iniquity is the *planning* of evil, and it is vile.

- Manipulation
- Affairs
- Abuses
- Living in lies
- Plotting to hurt others physically, emotionally, spiritually, or even socially

Iniquity is an ugly thing where the evil one cackles with delight, tainting, destroying, and shackling the doer to his or her destruction rather than experiencing the freedom and joy that await them in Christ. This sin stems from jealousy, insecurity, control issues, malice, hatred, and deceit. All things God's Word tells us to avoid.

Micah 2:1 says, "Woe to those who plan iniquity, to those who plot evil on their beds!" We have already covered that a woe is *a judgment or grief beyond description on a person or a group.* Why do you think he cast this woe? The answer actually is found in Isaiah 59:2. It says, "your iniquities have separated you from your God; your sins have hidden his face from you, so that he will not hear."

Woah. That is *serious*.

All sin separates us from God. When we realize we are sinners in need of a savior, we should repent. We should run to Jesus, the author of our salvation. We should stop living in sin and start living a life free in Christ. Paul, in Romans 6, takes this thought even further, check it out below.

What shall we say, then? Shall we go on sinning so that grace may increase? By no means! We are those who have died to sin; how can we live in it any longer? Or don't you know that all of us who were baptized into Christ Jesus were baptized into his death? We were therefore buried with him through baptism into death in order that, just as Christ was raised from the dead through the glory of the Father, we too may live a new life. For if we have been united with him in a death like his, we will certainly also be united with him in a resurrection like his. For we know that our old self was crucified with him so that the body ruled by sin might be done away with, that we should no longer be slaves to sin—because anyone who has died has been set free from sin (Romans 6:1–7).

My friend Jimmy is a fantastic all-around repair guy who was doing some electrical work for us just the other day. We began talking, and he shared his faith story. He became a believer as an adult, but in his high school days, he had lived life on the wild side. Cursing every few words or so was just his normal way of talking back then. As soon as he prayed the sinner's prayer, his first thought was, "I don't know how to talk!" What was so beautiful was that he wasn't bound by shame.

Jimmy just hadn't gotten saved—Jimmy *knew* he had been transformed! He had been so used to using curse words; he had to learn some new expressions because he had no desire to live the way he had been before Christ. Jimmy had been set free from sin, and he didn't want to talk like that ever again. He strived then, and still does today, to live in the ways of the Lord.

As Christians, we are called to live in God's will for our lives. Our Father God doesn't require perfection, but he does expect obedience. Repentance is not a one-time thing. It is a humble, daily conversation where we ask for God's strength to conquer sin in our lives. Why would we go on sinning and living in bondage when we have been set free by the blood of Jesus?

If Jesus is your Lord and Savior, he has freed you. You are no longer trapped by sin. The ropes have been loosened, the cords cut, the fence torn down. He rules our lives, and we freely and joyfully bind ourselves to his freedom and love.

Friends, I get it. It is no fun to slosh in the sludge of our lives and admit where we fail. It is important for our spiritual health to acknowledge and confess areas where we miss the mark, have crossed lines, or understand that we have justified sin through twisted, mortal reasoning. Sin is here to separate. Christ is here to reunite. Once we acknowledge sin, we can lay it down at the feet of our Savior and begin to walk in repentance, forgiveness, and salvation. Just like Jimmy.

I know these last few chapters have been intense, but grace and freedom await! We need to understand confession and repentance next, then we get into the joyful blessings and what is next as we live out our salvation. So, keep going, keep reading. It's worth all this introspection, I promise! Look, to use a gold bowl found in the dirt, you have to clean it first. This is us, digging out the dirt and scrubbing our hearts free from filth so the Lord can fill us with the many blessings that he has for us! Good things are coming, you guys!!!

Chapter Questions

How would you define *transgression* and *iniquity*?

How does each one "miss the mark" when it comes to the ways of God?

Chapter Six

THE TRUTH WILL
TAKE YOU OUT

Have you ever had a bad day with your spouse? Cory, my sweet husband, and I had one a few weeks ago when we found ourselves in a "heated discussion." Have you ever been there? We both were angry, but of the two of us, he held it together the best. I don't even remember what the fight was about, but, man, did it escalate quickly. And the fact that Cory was much calmer at one point than I was only added to my frustration and magnified my ugliness. I was trying to calm down but was still mad when I tried to apologize. My regret was half-hearted. I wanted to quit fighting but just wasn't ready to admit any wrong. Although I had apologized, there was no change in my actions or attitude.

Why am I telling you this?
Because that bad day is a good example of how *not* to confess a wrong.

Today, we are going to look into the importance of confession and then take on repentance. Those two things go hand in hand, and it is important for us to understand their correlation. *Merriam-Webster* defines confession as an acknowledgment of guilt by a party accused of an offense.[16] Repent, according to *Webster's 1828 Dictionary*, is a change in, or changing the course of, providential dealings.[17] The two verbs here are *acknowledgment* and *change*.

If we replace the words *confession* and *repent* with the less churchy forms of *acknowledgment* and *change*, we can see things a bit easier, just because these are words we use every day. Check out the sentences below:

- *Acknowledgment of sin* without planning to *change* is empty and meaningless.
- True, lasting *change* that lacks *acknowledgment* of sin is impossible.

Acknowledging our sin and changing our ways are necessary to bring us into a right relationship with God or other people. True confession comes from the heart and from the mouth. And when we repent, God begins to refresh our soul. God's Word tells us so. Check it out…

Whoever conceals their sins does not prosper, but the one who confesses and renounces them finds mercy. Blessed is the one who always trembles before God, but whoever hardens their heart falls into trouble (Proverbs 28:13–14).
Repent, then, and turn to God, so that your sins may be wiped out, that times of refreshing may come from the Lord (Acts 3:19).

If our desire is to be in the center of God's will, we must admit we are sinners and be aware of what those sins *are* so we can stop doing them. There should be a brokenness and grief over our sin, not just shallow acknowledgment that we have done something wrong. Confession should never be offered lightly or half-heartedly—it is the first step in moving back into a right relationship with the Lord.

Psalm 32:3–4 says, "When I kept silent, my bones wasted away through my groaning all day long. For day and night your hand was heavy on me; my strength was sapped as in the heat of summer."

There are all kinds of ways we can "waste away" because of sin. Physically, our bodies can be affected. Mentally, anxiety can take over and leave us feeling imbalanced, paranoid, and out of control. Socially, we can waste away because of fallout with friends and loved ones. Emotionally, we can become needy, distant, or hollow because sin has emptied out the spirit of joy and replaced it with pain. Unconfessed sin blocks us from the freedom of living out our salvation and finding comfort in our creator. Like Adam and Eve, sin makes us hide, cowering and afraid of the truth.

When I was a freshman in high school, *I* thought I was old enough to date. My *parents*, however, did not. I had a cute boy ask me to the movies, and we had a friend who had a boyfriend who would drive us—a double date! So, unbeknownst to my folks, we lined it up, and I thought I had covered all my tracks.

Friends, that night was awful. The guy was super nice, but I couldn't enjoy anything because I knew what I was doing was wrong. I had lied to my parents *and* the people I was with and was uneasy all night long. When I got home, things got even worse.

My mom was waiting for me in the den, sitting in a rocking chair facing the back door. I can hear the creak, creak, creak of the chair as I write this! Right as I walked in, I knew something was off. Mom, with a face of stone, asked where I'd been. *That* I could tell the truth on—I'd been to the movies. Then, she asked who I was with. I told her names.

The problem was, I told her the girl I was with had a brother that could drive. That "brother" in reality was her boyfriend. My mom got to the bottom of that pretty quick. Clearly, I had gone on a double date.

My mom had been fuzzy on the details and had called my friend's mom to make sure she didn't need to pick us up from the theater. Like they say, the truth always comes out. In this case, it *took me out* at the knees.

I didn't want to confess, and I wasn't about to repent and come home early. The funny thing was, I had already decided even before I was busted that I couldn't go on a date like that again. It was too much for my conscience. But when given the chance, I still didn't confess until I had gotten caught. My parents forgave me, but I was grounded for three weeks. I also had to memorize the Ten Commandments! I had learned a valuable lesson in telling the truth. The sin wasn't fun like I thought it would be. My parents reacted appropriately though—there was grace, and there was consequence for my actions.

Our God is a God of grace and mercy as well as judgment. Psalm 32:5 says that when we acknowledge our sin, quit covering our iniquity, and confess our transgressions, the Lord will forgive the guilt of my sin. Isn't that a beautiful thought? Confession and forgiveness are paired together in a lot of verses, because we must confess to fully receive forgiveness.

First John 1:9 says, "If we confess our sins, he is faithful and just and will forgive us our sins and purify us from all unrighteousness." Did you see that? Our Savior is *faithful* and *just* when we confess our sins to him. And did you see the two things he does for us? The Scripture says he will *forgive* us and *purify* us from unrighteousness.

Faithful and just.
Forgive and purify.

Isn't it crazy how in just one verse we see the amazing love of Jesus extended to us?

The Greek word translated in 1 John 1:9 as confess is the verb *homologeó*. It means to voice the same conclusion, to be in full agreement with, to acknowledge, to admit.[18]

When we confess our sin, we admit *in broken humility* that we are at fault. We stand in agreement with the Lord that our way is an abomination of his perfection. Confession is a refusal to be defined by our sin any longer. There is no padding or softening sin when true confession is at hand. Admitting our wrong is the first step in restoration. Without this acknowledgment, every additional step would be built on hollow intention.

There is a form of Japanese art called Kintsugi. It is a centuries-old technique that uses tree sap or lacquer dusted with gold to put broken pieces of pottery back together. Instead of attempting to conceal the brokenness of the pottery, it accentuates it with something even more beautiful and valuable than the pottery itself. With Kintsugi, the whole idea is to find beauty in the brokenness. The same concept can be applied when we confess our brokenness to the Lord.

Rest and healing are found in confession. When we admit our wrong, the Lord puts our lives back together and makes us even more beautiful than we were before. The brokenness of sin crumbles away, and we find ourselves put back together with God's love and restoration. The sin we are confessing is not news to our all-present and all-knowing God. He knows about it anyway, but we must acknowledge it and have a desire to change. Proverbs 28:13 tells us when we acknowledge our sins to God he offers mercy.

None of us are perfect, and we all have something to confess…

Every.
     Single.
          Day.

This idea of daily confession may be a new concept to you, but it is important if we want to keep transgressions and iniquity at bay. When we confess the small things and turn from them, those sins can't take root in our lives. The longer it takes us to confess, the tighter we get bound in our sin.

The story of David and Bathsheba is found in 2 Samuel 11. You may want to read it in full if you aren't familiar with it, but here are some things I'll point out for us to chew on if you are aware of the story...

Think how the story would be different if King David had confessed and repented about not going to war with his army (culturally, kings always went with their armies). He never would have ended up on the roof asking about Bathsheba. He would not have invited her over. He would not have slept with her. He would not have brought Uriah home from the front lines and gotten him drunk, trying to cover his tracks because David had gotten Uriah's wife pregnant. He would not have ordered Joab to put Uriah in a place where he was sure to be killed.

If David had made it a habit to confess and then repent every day, he would not have ended up an adulterer and a murderer.

If you don't mind writing in your book (or highlighting an electronic version), you can get a visual of the importance of daily confession. Underline each phrase and put a capital *C* for confession over each time David *could have* stopped from moving further into sin. Note the times he could have confessed and repented from his actions.

If David had focused on confession and repentance during those dark days, he could have avoided all kinds of evil. It is the same way in our lives. If we can focus on God's will, maintaining a spiritual alertness, we will save ourselves heartache and pain. Humble confession and repentance are stronger than any scheme of the devil.

What is in your life that you need to confess to the Lord? Remember, he knows it anyway, so this epiphany of sin may only be news to *you*.

First John 1:8 says, "If we claim to be without sin, we deceive our-selves and the truth is not in us." If you're up for a challenge, in the next twenty-four hours, ask the Lord to show you areas in your life where you need to confess and repent. Put this concept at the forefront of your mind. But be warned, this is dangerous. Our loving Savior will shine the light of his presence into the darkest parts of your soul and expose them to you. Focus not only on your actions but also on your attitudes, thoughts, opinions of others, maybe even of yourself. Let's tell him we don't want to be defined by these sins anymore. His grace, love, mercy, forgiveness, and freedom are waiting for us.

Chapter Questions

Have you ever had a time where you just weren't ready to confess a sin?

What was the process like that finally brought you to confession and repentance?

Chapter Seven

THE BENEFITS OF CONFESSION

This whole becoming *deeply defined* thing is easier said than done, isn't it?! Keep going, friends; we are almost to the wide-open spaces of forgiveness, freedom, joy, grace, and more that the Lord wants to pour into our hearts. The gut-wrenching topics of sin, confession, and repentance are almost behind us! But first, like a good spring cleaning, we've got to scrub away the dirt that could be clogging or slowing the movement of God in our lives. We've got to be incredibly honest with ourselves and deeply aware of where we are in our spiritual lives.

I am writing this on a plane coming home from a women's retreat at the beach. The weather was perfect, the ladies were precious, and we dug deep into the word of God together. I am blessed and happy, but I am tired. It is *late*. I've got an hour's drive after we land before my head can hit the pillow, and it's going to be past midnight when I get home. I must stay alert as I drive. That word *alert* reminds me of something the apostle Peter talks about in his first letter.

First Peter 5:8–10 says, "Be alert and of sober mind. Your enemy the devil prowls around like a roaring lion looking for someone to devour. Resist him, standing firm in the faith, because you know that the family of believers throughout the world is undergoing the same kind of sufferings. And the God of all grace, who called you to his eternal glory in Christ, after you have suffered a little while, will himself restore you and make you strong, firm, and steadfast."

To really make the above verses pop, I want to point out some things. Peter lists off four things we should be or do when we resist the devil.

1. We should be alert.
2. We should be of sober mind.
3. We should resist him.
4. We should stand firm in our faith.

After all, like the verse says, the devil is looking for someone to devour. Don't let that be you.

Do you see the four things it says God provides after we undergo our sufferings? It says God will…

1. Restore you.
2. Make you strong.
3. Help you stand firm.
4. Lead you to be steadfast.

I want all that. Don't you? In these verses from 1 Peter, we immediately see how we should be on our guard, as the devil wants to drag us down. Our good God desires to lift us up. One way the evil one can keep us in the demolition zone is by making our hearts hard, or just dull, so we will *not* confess our sins. He can do this through busyness, stubbornness, or even ignorance.

In confession, we see God's perfection and our imperfection. When we admit our sins, our earthly goals no longer matter. His will and ways take precedence in our minds and hearts. We begin to stand on the solid ground of faith in Christ. True, heartfelt confession is humility at its best.

Authentic confession is followed by a change in action to stop the sin at hand.

James 4:8 tells us how to be authentic in confession. We are to draw near to God, cleanse our hands, and purify our hearts. When we join this verse with the idea of confession and repentance, we see submission to God and a freedom from sin for us.

Yesterday, I realized I was harboring hurt toward a few people who had caused me great emotional pain. For a long time, I responded by praying for them, that they would know the Lord, be more loving, and find joy and freedom in Christ. But I also had been complaining to Cory about the pain they were causing me... a lot. I had been praying for them, *but not for myself.*

How often do we do that? I had chosen to live in hurt rather than true and complete forgiveness. That, friends, is sin. My heart needed to be purified through drawing near to God and confessing my sin. After tears and laying my sin before the Lord, I felt a weight lifted off, replaced by a new perspective of mercy, love, and even a joy of learning a lesson in Christ. Proverbs 28:13 says, "Whoever conceals their sins does not prosper, but the one who confesses and renounces them find mercy."

Mercy.
I want that from the Father.
I bet you do to.

You may be strong in your faith at the moment or you may be in denial and up to your eyeballs in sin. You might be where I was, able to see the sin in others who have hurt you but not in your attitude of sin toward them. Let's stop and recognize any sins that are blocking us from seeing God fully. Don't you want those removed?

Since none of us are perfect, we all have something to confess. It is one-sided to worship with hands held high yet fold our arms in refusal when we are asked to confront sin in our lives. If we are open in worship, then we must be open in confession. Confession is a part of worship.

Start by lifting your hands up in a prayer of thanksgiving and praise. Take a moment to worship the Lord in his holiness and feel the glory of his presence in your life. Go to him humbly with a contrite heart. Isn't the meaning deeper since you know the true definition of these words? Think of some attributes of his character and worship him for who he is in your life.

Now, stop and think about how you've been living your life this week. What have your actions, words, and attitudes been like? How could they line up better with the greatest commandment, which, according to Matthew 22:36–40, is to love God and love others?

Compare those actions, words, and attitudes with those of Christ. Don't justify ungodly attitudes (they "made me" act like that; "I can't stand her"; "it's just how I deal with things"), but humbly see them for what they are—sin that is keeping you from the freedom God desires for your life.

Confess to our loving Father any thought, attitude, or action you have that is not in line with his Spirit. Are you angry because of hurt? Are you living in fear and not freedom? Are you self-centered rather than Christ-centered? Are you choosing to live in hate, rather than repentance and freedom in Christ? Oh friend, if you hold on to that hate, you are putting that over Christ, making that an idol. Be as specific as you can be as you talk to God, humbly admitting your wrong and asking the Lord to strengthen you to do what is right.

Look, we can't manufacture contriteness. If it's not there, ask God to begin to break your heart for him if nothing else. And let me tell you—when I ask this, he does it every time.

Finally, make an action plan for how you are going to repent and change. Be specific not only in what you are going to do to turn from your sin but also in what you are going to do to put up guardrails to help you not fall into that same sin again.

Unfortunately, many times sin is bigger than we are, but it is *never* bigger than the One *in* us. Confession is acknowledging and taking responsibility for our actions. Repentance is choosing and committing to change those actions. Both are needed if we want to live in the freedom of Christ.

Chapter Question

Why is confession such an important discipline for all of us?

Chapter Eight

THE IMPORTANCE OF REPENTANCE

Hey there, I know this may not be easy reading. It can be emotional, and even a bit overwhelming, when God reveals something in our lives that should not be there. It is worth the struggle, as freedom awaits. I don't know about you, but most Christmases, my pants get a little tight. The fudge, the cookies, the cheesiness of all the casseroles, it makes my clothes shrink a bit. But that helps me realize I need to tighten up my diet, skip some desserts, and get some exercise. It's a wake-up call that I need to work some stuff out. That's where we are with confession and repentance. You may be feeling a little tight or a little squeezed, so let's work it out together.

I hope you've chosen to open your heart in confession. I want us to go even deeper into what that can mean for us. John Owen, an English theologian who lived in the 1600s, said if you're not about killing sin, then "it will be killing you."[19]

I hope you are in the process of slaughtering whatever sin is keeping you from a closer relationship with the Lord. My desire is for you to walk away with a renewed awareness of the Holy Spirit in your life. I want you to move forward in freedom and confidence and distance yourself even more from whatever it is that could be weighing you down.

To jump right in, confession takes us to the cross where the chains of shame can be unlocked by Jesus, the key to our hope and salvation. Admitting our sin releases a sense of humility and freedom, allowing us to stare in wonder at the personal, awesome forgiveness of our Heavenly Father. We then can define ourselves through God's eyes, not by explaining away the shortcomings of our sin.

Repentance, a turning away from wrong, completes the step of confession. It can be like making a U-turn on a map. Or it can be a smaller course correction if you catch it before you get too off track.

My friend Jess has a thirteen-year old daughter named Kinley, who is bubbly, cute as a button, and great at math. Jess just found out that every day, for the last *two years*, Kinley's bedside clock has been wrong. *Way* wrong. Seven-hours-and-two-minutes-behind-the-correct-time wrong. You know what Kinley has been doing about it?

Instead of taking thirty seconds to fix the numbers, she has been adding seven hours and two minutes every time she looks at the clock. Before bed, math. Middle of the night, math. In the morning if she awoke before Jess came in to wake her, math. What can we learn from Kinley? Way more than math! The last two years of Kinley's life show us that if we correct ourselves when we get off track, life will be much easier.

A godly adjustment, correction, or change enables us to walk forward with confidence. We need to celebrate when we break free from sin, no matter how small it may seem. We then need to commit to healing through the power of Jesus in our lives.

Jesus preached a lot about repentance. Mark 1:14–15 and Matthew 4:17 both show us that Jesus started his ministry with the message of "repent." Repentance was a main theme of his teaching his whole time on earth. But these verses have one thing that is a little different than the other:

- Matthew 4:17 says to repent because the kingdom of heaven is near.
- Mark 1:14–15 says to repent because the kingdom of God is near.

Let's stop and understand the biblical culture in which these two books were written. Jesus is talking about the same concept in both these phrases, but his listeners were from different cultures. The Jewish audience of the day would say "Kingdom of Heaven" and never, ever use the term "Kingdom of God." Even in today's culture, many practicing Jews actually write "G-d" rather than "God" out of reverence and respect. It is a willful act of carefulness to never take the name of the Lord in vain, even by accident.

The newly converted Greek or other non-Jewish Christ followers in Jesus's day would call it the Kingdom of God. This wasn't out of a lack of respect but simply because they weren't coming out of the Jewish culture that had deep roots in reverence for the Jewish God. Either way, and no matter what the phrase, the message is clear. Jesus said repent because his kingdom was near.

And what is his kingdom? It is made up of the people who call him Lord. Like the fictional character of Lord Grantham of *Downton Abbey* or the not as suave but just as entertaining Lord Farquaad in *Shrek*, these lords were in charge of those around them. It was their land and their village that their people lived and worked. The people under these lords did what they were told because the "Lord of the Land" was in charge.

Jesus reigns in our lives as Lord when we admit we are sinners, believe he is God's son, and confess our sins and our need for him. We live in his kingdom, and he is Lord over us. Because he is our Lord, we are never alone and never outside of his kingdom's reign.

John Piper refers to repentance as "an internal change of mind and heart rather than mere sorrow for sin or mere improvement of behavior."

He points out the Greek word translated as repent, *metanoeo*, has two parts: *meta* and *noeo*.

The prefix meta means movement or change.
Noeo refers to the mind, its thoughts, perceptions, dispositions and purposes.

So, "repent" can be defined as a change of mind, purpose, or attitude.[20]

In Hebrew, the word *teshuvah* is translated as repent. It literally means "to return," as in doing a 180-degree turn and going back to where you were before. It paints a picture of someone seeing with new eyes what has been left behind and replacing a new, healthy relationship with one that was old and broken. Have you ever wished you could go back a day, a week, a year and change a bad decision? You were wishing for teshuvah, a renewal of the way things used to be before sin entered the picture.

We see this clearly in the story of the prodigal son. Teshuvah is not just feeling bad about a sin. It is *the outward result of making a decision to turn away from sin* and start anew.[21] We must understand that confession, without turning away from sin, does us no good whatsoever. We must confess our sins and then turn from them to live the way God intended.

Isaiah 55:7 (NLT) says, "Let the wicked *change* their ways and banish the very *thought* of doing wrong. Let them *turn* to the Lord that he may have mercy on them. Yes, turn to our God for he will forgive generously."

One of Satan's best lies is getting us to believe we aren't wicked. The word *wicked* is usually reserved for horrible people—murderers, idolaters, the exceptionally bad eggs. If we think we are doing okay, or at least better than those around us, why would we need to confess, much less repent? But our scale of good and bad is not an earthly one. We can't compare ourselves to others—this brings everything from pride to depression—but, instead, we should let Christ be our example of how to live. The Hebrew word for wicked, *rasha*, is nothing extreme. It simply means one guilty of a crime, one deserving punishment.[22]

Well, *that* changes things, doesn't it?

All of us have sinned; all of us have fallen short of the glory of God (Romans 3:23). Aren't you thankful for the gift of grace and redemption that is found in Christ Jesus (Romans 3:24)? As sinners, we *all* are wicked; we *all* deserve punishment because we *all* have broken God's commands. Jesus's constant message of repentance was to unlock the chains of sin and bring the freedom that comes from salvation through him. Confession helps us see life with a renewed outlook, and repentance is a commitment to live differently in that outlook.

Isaiah 55:7 gives us some great advice: The wicked (one deserving punishment) should abandon their ways. The sinful one (who missed the mark) should abandon his thoughts. We all (that's us) should return to the Lord.

And Isaiah doesn't just tell us what he thinks we should do; he tells us the benefits we get when we do the right thing. It says when we return to the Lord, he will have compassion on us. Isn't that beautiful? Even though we fell short, even though we are guilty of deserving punishment, God is still there with his compassion to love and forgive.

Our Father is a God of mercy, forgiveness, hope, and freedom. We will not experience those blessings when we choose to defy his will and live in sin. The closer we follow the Lord, the more we confess and repent, the more freedom and joy we will have because we will be less bound by sin in our lives.

Being aware of what it right isn't enough. There are sins of commission, which are sins we take part in, and there are sins of omission, which is knowing what is right and not doing it. James 4:17 makes the concept of sin of omission clear when we read, "If anyone, then, knows the good they ought to do and doesn't do it, it is sin for them." What does that mean with confession and repentance? If we know we are wrong, we must confess and repent. When we refuse to do that out of pride, hard-heartedness, or just plain old stupidity, we pile on to the already existing mess in our lives.

The short of it is you now know the importance of confession and repentance. You now know what they mean practically, as well as in three languages. It is your choice if you will implement them into your life.

Acts 3:19 tells us to repent and turn back so our sins can be wiped away. If you are willing, ask the Lord to give you strength and wisdom as you turn from sin in your life, no matter how small. None of us are perfect, and we all have junk. We all need to seek the Lord in humility every single day. Our whole life should be a personal journey of holiness. Pray about instituting daily confession and repentance in your life. Journal on a sheet of paper how you think it could strengthen you in your walk with the Lord and tuck it away in your Bible as a reminder.

Chapter Question

How can daily confession and repentance help you stay on track spiritually?

Chapter Nine

FORGIVENESS... NO, REALLY!

O ne of the most heartbreaking conversations I've ever had was with a vibrant, intelligent Christian woman who had made some mistakes in her life. With tears streaming down her face, she explained that God could not forgive her for what she had done. She couldn't even form a sentence of what her sin had been; she would crumble each time she tried. When I assured her that God would and could forgive her, she still would not accept that God's love was bigger than her sin. She was shattered before the Lord and had confessed and repented but continued to stay bound in by guilt when God had already set her free.

Friends, please don't hold on to guilt when God has released you from the chains of shame and sin. It is for freedom that Christ set us free, and oh how he wants you to be free! For us to be defined by our Savior, and *not* our sin, all we have to do is humbly admit where we are wrong and change our ways. It really is that simple. After that, we *can* experience forgiveness without holding on to guilt or shame. If you struggle with accepting God's forgiveness, understand that you have been created for a reason and a purpose—and neither of those is for you to be bound in sin.

James 2:10 reads, "For whoever keeps the whole law and yet stumbles at just one point is guilty of breaking all of it." This puts all sin on the same level. It makes us feel better to see a "little white lie" and murder as two distinct failures—and they do have two distinct forms of justice—but both have the same result: separation from the Lord.

Everyone is a sinner. Everyone has separated himself or herself from the Lord. We all need to confess and repent of our guilt so we can experience God's forgiveness. Our sin does not define us…

Unless

we

just

can't

let

it

go.

Jesus died to save us from our sin, be it what the world deems as big or small. The Lord sees us all with the same desire—that we know him and the one he sent (John 17:3). God sees your good days and bad days. He knows the deepest part of your soul. His desire is for you to search and know him deeply in return.

Jesus knew the woman at the well had gone through five husbands but loved her anyway. He knew Judas would betray him yet loved him anyway. He loved tax collectors and sinners and nobodies and somebodies. That thing you did? Jesus knows. And he loves you anyway. While on earth, Jesus loved others because he knew the importance of forgiveness. He still knows it today. So, what is forgiveness? The definition, as we usually understand it, is a restoration of a relationship that entails the removal of guilt.[23]

In Hebrew, however, it goes a little deeper. A word that appears over six hundred times in the Bible is *nasa*, and it's just one of the Hebrew words I want you to learn about. Nasa means to "lift, carry, or forgive."[24] In Daniel 2:35, the author uses the term *nasa* to show how chaff gets carried away by the wind. The chaff must be separated from the wheat so the wheat can be utilized and enjoyed. The chaff is worthless, but the wheat is important.

The last time I was in Israel, our group visited Katzrin, a replica of a Talmudic village. Katzrin was a real village in the fourth century, and parts of it have been restored. Man, did we have a blast! We started out by putting on clothing the way it would have been worn in biblical times. We baked and ate pita bread outside on an open metal dome, with an interested peacock watching hungrily nearby. We saw an old wine press and ruins of the town synagogue, where we accidentally crashed a bar mitzvah, which they loved because we were in our "Jesus clothes," and we loved as well because we had never seen one before. It was a win-win!

Also, while at Katzrin, we learned how to separate the wheat from its chaff. A few from our group did this with a wooden type of pitchfork. There were also large, round, flat baskets for us to try out. The wheat went inside the basket, and we were told to toss it over and over again. There was a nice breeze that day, and we could actually see the chaff blowing away into the wind. The chaff was rice-paper thin and would blow and twist and turn with the gusts, being taken away with the breeze. The more we tossed, the more was lifted and carried away. What a beautiful picture of what God does with our sin!

Can you think of a time when God lifted your burden and carried your sin away with his forgiveness? What did it feel like to be free, feeling the glory (weight) of God's presence and forgiveness rather than the weight of your sin? It's an amazing feeling, isn't it, to know that we have been forgiven by one who is perfect. That we can be with him, blessed by him, when we simply submit to his will.

Another Hebrew word for forgiveness is *kaphar*, and it means "to cover, atone for sin."[25] In Genesis 6, God tells Noah to build an ark. One of the instructions God gives our aquatic friend is to *kaphar* the ark with pitch inside and out. I imagine when Noah did this he wasn't satisfied with one thin layer since he knew he would be there a while. I bet it was thick and sticky, assuring that the ark would be waterproof. And we see this Hebrew word again in the book of Isaiah when the angel touched Isaiah's lips with the burning coal in the throne room. The angel told Isaiah his sins were covered. Isaiah didn't act like this covering was a light dusting of forgiveness either; he knew the depth of his sin and the width of this covering.

A third Hebrew word we need to understand comes from the verb *salach*. It means "to forgive, pardon."[26] In 1 Samuel 15:24–25 (ESV), King Saul asks to be pardoned after the Lord rejected him. To be pardoned means a person is released from punishment. This version of forgive shows there should not be a spirit of reciprocation by us when forgiveness comes into play. This is the opposite idea of an eye for an eye. The forgiven party is pardoned from guilt and punishment is withheld.

Has there been a time in your life when God withheld punishment for a sin you committed, simply out of his grace and forgiveness? When we know we are guilty of something, yet God gives us forgiveness and grace, it can be a powerful moment of worship. That grace given is not because of anything we have done but simply because of who he is to us. God is a God of forgiveness, and that forgiveness is full of mercy, grace, love, and second chances.

To sum things up, our Hebrew words show us that forgiveness can be defined in a few different ways:

- God lifts and carries our burdens of guilt and shame (*nasa*).
- God covers and atones our worry, insecurity, and fear (*kaphar*).
- God pardons us when we turn and seek his face (*salach*).

In the New Testament, the Greek word for forgive, *aphiemi*, has two parts. The first part of the word, *apo*, means "away from." The second part of the word, *hiemi*, means "send away." If you switch those around and blend them together, we come up with the meaning "send away from." *Aphiemi* can also mean "to leave alone, permit to depart, and even suffer."[27] The idea here of forgiveness is that the wrong has been sent away from the relationship, not sticking around to be brought up again.

Your sin may be bigger than you, but it is not bigger than God. If you struggle with accepting this truth, that sentence needs to become foundational in your life. Take a moment and ask God to help you understand his love. Pray daily until it becomes a reality in your life.

Because of Jesus, our sin is

- carried away;
- covered;
- pardoned;
- and separated from us.

We are forgiven and not defined by our sin anymore. Christ brings freedom. Christ brings redemption. In Christ, there is forgiveness of any sin we have committed. Acts 13:38–39 says, "Therefore, my friends, I want you to know that through Jesus the forgiveness of sins is proclaimed to you. Through him everyone who believes is set free from every sin, a justification you were not able to obtain under the law of Moses."

Christ has set you free. Go, and live like it.

Chapter Question

What are the similarities and differences in the four different words for forgiveness?

Chapter Ten

FORGIVENESS, AGAIN

I n the past few chapters, we have been laser-focused on ourselves, working through *our* sin, *our* shame, *our* mistakes. Now we will finish discussing forgiveness but in how we offer it to others. Extending forgiveness deepens our faith by allowing us to experience grace as the giver, not the receiver. Forgiveness is love lived out in one of its purest forms, and it can be really, really hard. Our relationship with Jesus is not just about God *in* us, but God working *through* us.

It was C. S. Lewis who said, "To be a Christian means to forgive the inexcusable because God has forgiven the inexcusable in you."[28] When we confess and repent, God forgives our sins. *Every. Single. Time.* Forgiveness is beautiful and gentle and humbling. It is given when we are weak because we have offended, made a mistake, or been overtaken by sin. It is only in the strength of Christ and depth of faith that we are able to offer that same love and spirit of forgiveness to others.

Tray and Melody looked like a perfect couple. They met at a private Christian university and married right after Melody graduated. Ten years later, with four kids under the age of five, life began to crumble. Unbeknownst to Melody, Tray had been struggling with a porn addiction since he was a child.

He hid his addiction by going to chat rooms online, but, eventually, virtual sex turned into reality and led to multiple affairs. Tray and Melody read books and went to counseling, but nothing could fix the brokenness they both felt in their hearts.

Their marriage ended in divorce.

Both felt helpless. Both tried to move on. Melody even remarried for a time, but that marriage didn't last long. After a few years, Tray was at the beach with his kids. One of his sons came up asking for help with an infected toe. Tray knew he was going to have to lance it and said something to the effect of "I can fix your toe, but Daddy has to make it hurt before it can heal."

Tray says, at that moment, that he knew God was saying the same thing to him. It was a turning point. He realized that all pain isn't negative, and he was going to have to walk through healing pain by himself and with Melody if there was going to be resolution between the two of them.

They both began to engage life with more strength, and they lived in vulnerability. They learned to do life from a new perspective that operated in truth and open communication. They found a new groove and after a while, Tray and Melody remarried... each other!

What had been undone was now redone, and that is where the title of their ministry comes from. They both understand forgiveness from the side of the giver and the receiver. They now have been remarried longer than they were divorced, and both personify forgiveness in their marriage. They worked through the pain and were healed. (Note: Tray and Melody have a ministry where they lead conferences and speak to churches. If you'd like to have them at yours, check out their website, UndoneRedone.com or email them at Melody@UndoneRedone.com.)

The reality is… if we can't forgive, we can't heal. When the love we should have for others is tainted by a wrong they have done, our hearts battle with the thought of forgiveness. But we have received forgiveness from the Lord.

In our pain, we don't want to forgive, but we must.

Maybe your pain stems from marital unfaithfulness. The way you were treated by a friend or coworker. Your family of origin. Or maybe it comes from jealousy of someone else's family, or social status, or appearance. You don't want to forgive people for seemingly having it easier than you. A lack of forgiveness gone unchecked can lead to feelings of hate.

People refuse to forgive for all kinds of things and end up hating for all kinds of reasons. Many times, the hated don't deserve the hate felt toward them. Whatever the reason, if a sinful attitude goes unchecked, it will grow. Our unforgiveness can get judgmental. Bitter. Resentful. And if those attitudes continue to grow, it can lead to hate.

First John 2:9–11 says, "Anyone who claims to be in the light but hates a brother or sister is still in the darkness. Anyone who loves their brother and sister lives in the light, and there is nothing in them to make them stumble. But anyone hates his brother or sister is in the darkness and walks around in the darkness. They do not know where they are going, because the darkness has blinded them." When someone hates another, John tells us they live in symbolic darkness. Darkness in the Bible always represents sin.

Hating another person is sin. We can't get around this, and we can't allow hate to enter our heart. Just as light and dark can't exist in the same space, neither can our love for God nor hate for his creation.

Maybe you don't deal with hate. Hate, after all, is a very big word. Your struggle could be with offering mercy to someone who wronged you. But remember, if we receive it from the Lord, we must be willing to give it to others.

The book of Matthew records Jesus and Peter having a conversation about forgiveness that echoes with an attitude of mercy. Peter leads with the huge number of seven, inquiring if that is enough times to forgive someone. That sounds like a merciful number, doesn't it? I wonder what the look on both their faces was when Jesus countered back, no Peter, not seven. You need to forgive someone seventy-seven times! Jesus's point is if we truly comprehend his forgiveness, we will extend that same forgiveness to others.

James 2:12–13 echoes the point found in Matthew. To nutshell it, these verses say we should speak and act like we are going to be judged… because we *are* going to be judged. If we don't show mercy to others, mercy will not be shown to us.

Maybe you don't struggle with hatred *or* offering mercy when you have been wronged. Maybe what is holding back your forgiveness is a judgmental attitude. This is a tough one because we hide behind our "Christian nice" and tuck this mindset into the ugly depths of some secret self. But if we look, we know it's there, and so does our Creator. A judgmental attitude can bind us and keep us from offering forgiveness. Why?

Because

we

can't

get

over

ourselves.

Matthew 7:1–2 says, "Do not judge, or you too will be judged. For in the same way you judge others, you will be judged, and with the measure you use, it will be measured to you." If you struggle with offering forgiveness to someone, personalize this verse and ask yourself, What measure of judgment am I using for this person right now? Is my heart hardened toward someone? Am I okay with the Lord judging me/treating me like I judge/treat [___]?

Matthew 6:14–15 is pretty clear. It says, "For if you forgive other people when they sin against you, your heavenly Father will also forgive you. But if you do not forgive others their sins, your Father will not forgive your sins."

That's pretty clear, isn't it?

Yes, forgiveness can be difficult. But again, we must look to Jesus, the author and perfecter of our faith. When he had gone through an illegal trial, been tortured, beaten, and left alone and hanging on the cross, Jesus said, "Father, forgive them, for they do not know what they are doing" (Luke 23:34).

Jesus models for us to:

Love one another.
Show mercy.
Not judge.
Forgive.

Colossians 3:13 says, "Bear with each other and forgive one another if any of you has a grievance against someone. Forgive as the Lord forgave you."

We are to forgive the way the Lord forgives us each and every day. That creates a sense of humility, doesn't it? It's a constant reminder that we aren't perfect. Because we receive mercy and forgiveness from God, we are capable of extending it to others. Isn't it wonderful to be defined as a forgiver because of the gift of our Father? Through Jesus's death on the cross and the gift of his Holy Spirit in our lives, he has *empowered us* to be like him.

What about offering forgiveness when something isn't just bad but evil? Some of you sweet friends reading this have been violated in ways that have left a pain so deep, you feel you will never get over what was done to you. To forgive doesn't always mean you have to restore a relationship, and it may be unhealthy for you to do so.

Forgiveness breaks the chains of bitterness, insecurity, anger, resentment, and fear. If that sin done to you has defeated you, let me assure you, it cannot defeat God. He is bigger than any sin that has been committed against you. He can conquer the effects of that sin and bring freedom and joy back into your life. If you haven't already, let someone help you work through your pain. Don't let those actions done to you keep you bound in shame. You are a child of the King, beautiful one. Let Jesus set you free.

To experience freedom in Christ, we must experience forgiveness—both in offering it and receiving it. If you find that you are struggling with unforgiveness in your heart, begin to focus daily on the people you need to forgive in your prayer time. If you can't forgive, then ask the Lord to give you the strength to begin to heal and be able to let go of your pain. As you heal, forgiveness will come by the Lord's power. Keep pursuing it; we are commanded to do so. It can be hard, but freedom in Christ is incredibly worth it.

Here are some prayer tips to help you get started:

- Thank the Lord for forgiving your sins.
- Pray daily to have a forgiving attitude.
- Ask for love, grace, and mercy, and for the ability to see others as Christ does.
- Ask God to remove any resentment, judgmental attitudes, bitterness, unmerciful mindsets, pain, fear, insecurity, anxiety, and other ill effects that a committed sin against you has brought on. Ask the Lord to help you move into the freedom of trusting his heart.

- If the person who wronged you is not a Christian, pray that person will be transformed by the salvation found only in Jesus Christ.

Chapter Question

Reread Colossians 3:13. How does the idea of forgiveness compare with the verses on hate, judging, and mercy?

Chapter Eleven

HOW MERCY DIFFERS FROM GRACE

The last few mornings, even before my eyes have opened, God has been whispering part of Lamentations 3:22–23 (ESV) deep into my brain. I think it's the Lord wanting me to share it with you. It says, "The steadfast love of the Lord never ceases; his mercies never come to an end; they are new every morning; great is your faithfulness."

Did you catch that? It says God's mercies *never* come to an end. Can you think of a more beautiful picture?

The concepts of grace and mercy are kind of like *The Property Brothers*, the fix-it-up guys on reality TV. They look similar because they are twins, but they are two very different and distinct people. Now, if you asked me which one was Drew and which one was Jonathan, I don't have a clue. A lot of people have a similar confusion with grace and mercy.

It's important to grasp that grace and mercy are two distinct concepts because we need to celebrate their differences. Their similarity can't be denied, yet it's in the subtle nuance where we find deeper meaning and thankfulness. These next few chapters will focus on both grace and mercy so we can untangle them and then apply them to our lives.

A short contrast is that mercy is withholding a deserved consequence, whereas grace is extended favor for no reason other than the giver's own character and compassion.

- Mercy = Withholding
- Grace = Extending

Hebrews 4:16 describes God's throne as a throne of grace. It says from that throne we can *receive* mercy and *find* grace. The favor God extends to us is not because of anything we have done but because of who he is. Grace is flowing, mercy is given.

Mercy is not making us pay the price for our sin. Grace is Jesus paying for our sin in full. Forrest Gump would say they go together like peas and carrots. Both of these come out of an extended loving-kindness to us from our Creator, which brings us to the Hebrew word *chesed* (pronounced HEH-sid with a guttural *H*). In my opinion, this is one of the best words in the Bible. Chesed is too big to be translated into one English word. We don't have it in our vocabulary.

In chesed, we find compassion and mercy. Forgiveness. Kindness. Love and grace. All rolled into who the Creator is toward his creation. Chesed describes who God is, *as well as* the lens he sees us through. Isn't that beautiful? An act of chesed presupposes a relationship between two people when no previous relationship is there. The person showing chesed has chosen to treat the receiver as if a close relationship already existed.[29]

The Hebrew word *chesed* can be defined as mercy or loving-kindness. It is close to grace but has a twist. Mercy is undeserved favor flowing with compassion from a superior to an inferior, with an element of withholding what is deserved.[30] The *Oxford Dictionary* clarifies even more when we add its definition of mercy—"compassion or forgiveness shown toward someone whom it is within one's power to punish or harm."[31] The Greek word for mercy, *eleos*, is defined as "mercy, compassion, active pity, with the sense of goodness in general, especially piety."[32] This word also is used to describe God.

Sometimes to understand what something is, you can learn what it is *not*. Deuteronomy 4:31 tells us:

- God will not abandon us.
- God will not destroy us.
- God will not forget the covenant he made with us.

Not to focus on the negative, but that is positive stuff! Knowing the God of the Universe will not leave us is big. Knowing that he is not out to get us, and he will always remember that he saved us is massive. Our God is a covenant God who does not change his mind. But sometimes our minds get sidetracked, don't they? We say we want him to be first in our hearts, but life gets in the way and hardens our souls. God is always there though, offering grace and mercy so we can run back to him.

Even though the Israelites had wandered forty years in the desert, the Lord never left them. He never broke his covenant with them. He was a pillar of cloud by day and a pillar of fire at night, guiding them every step of the way. Have you ever stopped to ponder how thoughtful God was in the way he showed his presence to his people? That cloud offered shade in the hot desert. It's not like there were a lot of trees around to rest under; it was a *desert*.

And that pillar of fire, not only did it offer light but warmth for the cool desert nights. The people may have been wandering in the desert, but the Lord knew where they were the whole time. He was graciously providing for them every step of the way. If you feel you have wandered from the Lord, friend, please know he is there, waiting to accept you back into a relationship with him. His mercies are new every morning.

He hasn't saved us based on our deeds. He saved us by grace and by his mercy.

And just as we have received mercy, we are to extend it to others. I'm sure you've heard the expression "You can't give what you don't have." Have you ever noticed it's easiest to be kind when people are kind to you? If you are a Christian, God has granted you mercy again and again. Likewise, we must extend mercy to those around us—whether they are kind or not. If we accept something so beautiful from the Lord yet refuse to extend it to our fellow man, our actions are self-focused, shallow, and entitled. If you accept God's mercy in your own life, you must be willing to extend it to others.

In Matthew 18 we find the parable of the unmerciful servant. The way Jesus told it, there was a king who was updating his accounts, seeing who owed him money. He found a man who owed him millions of dollars. When the man was brought to the king, he couldn't pay his debt. The king was going to sell the debtor and his family in order to pay what he owed, but the man begged for mercy. The king not only granted the man's request but forgave his debt. However, as soon as this man was out of the king's company, he marched straight over to someone who owed him a few thousand dollars. He started choking the guy and demanded payment! That person begged for mercy, but instead of giving it, he had the man thrown into prison.

Some servants saw the whole thing and reported all that had happened back to the king. Infuriated, the king had the man brought back into his presence. He called him *evil* because he refused to have mercy on his fellow man. The king then redacted his former mercy and forgiveness of debt and instead had the man sent to prison where he was going to be tortured until he could pay every penny. And then Jesus ends the story with this mic drop:

This is how my heavenly Father will treat each of you unless you forgive your brother or sister from your heart.

Did you see how Jesus said we must forgive from the heart? That is full-fledged forgiveness, my friend. Forgiveness can't come out of our mouths when bitterness stays in our souls. For us to be truly merciful, we must forgive from the core of our being. If this seems like too big of a task for you, that's okay. It is never too big for the Lord! Begin to pray that you will be able to offer mercy to those who have wronged you. Ask for God's power to reveal itself through mercy in your life. It is not easy, but the freedom you will feel is worth it in the end.

Luke 6:36 (NTE) doesn't mince any words when talking about mercy and compassion either. It says, "You must be merciful, just as your father is merciful." Did you see the word *must*? We can't ignore the command to offer mercy, even if we want to. The Greek word used for merciful in this verse is referring to the attitude of expressing compassion for someone. That is so hard to do when we feel wronged, isn't it? As Christians, we don't have a choice. We have to struggle and strive and learn to be merciful. With the Lord's help, we can do it, you guys!

Matthew 5:7 continues to show us why we should fight for this attitude in our hearts. It says, "Blessed are the merciful, for they will be shown mercy." I hate to admit it, but there have been times in my life where I have been a complete jerk. Have you ever been there? I am incredibly thankful the Lord does not hold those times against me, or you, and instead offers his love and mercy into our broken times of stupidity and shame. I'm so thankful we serve a God who loves us despite our past and our mistakes.

So far, we have seen Jesus tell us we "must" be merciful and that the merciful are "blessed." And, if the fact that we should live a life of mercy isn't clear enough, the book of Micah tells us that the Lord requires some things of us.

That we are required to act justly, to love mercy, and to walk humbly with our God.

A requirement.
Not a choice.

When we need or want mercy from others, we understand the weight of it. When others need it from us and we don't give it, our hearts are hard and mercy is denied. The Lord *requires* mercy from us. If we choose to receive it from the Lord, giving it to others is not optional. It is not up to us, our mood, or our opinion. If Satan can convince us we don't have to offer mercy, he can stop the church in its tracks.

Micah 6:8 all goes together by the way—acting justly *is* to love mercy, which *is* to walk humbly with our God. It's a package deal. It's a direction of how we should live. So, live today knowing that our God has had mercy on you. Relish it. Be saturated by it. And since you have received mercy freely, be sure you are extending it freely to others.

Chapter Questions

How would you define grace and mercy? How they are the same, and how they are different?

Chapter Twelve

ENCOURAGED BY GRACE

B ecause Cory and I admire and respect the great theologian Charles Spurgeon, we have given him a nickname. His writings have impacted us immensely, and we feel like he is a personal friend of ours in some crazy way. Thus, we call him (read it with a cool kind of low drawl)… "Spuuuurge." Spurge said many things worth a quote, things that are deep and spiritual and meaningful. One of my favorites, however, I am going to paraphrase. It's from a sermon he gave in the balmy summer of 1888. It's timeless, true, and right on point.

He basically said if someone thinks you're a bad person, don't worry about it. You are *way* worse than they—or you—realize.[33]

Spuuuurrrge.
Always the encourager.

But here's the deal: He's *right*. We are all sinners, saved by grace (Ephesians 2:8–10). When we realize that, our whole viewpoint of ourselves and others is radically changed.

- The gift of grace diminishes discouragement because there is forgiveness.
- The gift of grace means mistakes don't define us because there is hope.
- The gift of grace renews us regularly because there is salvation.

Isaiah 30:18 tells us that the Lord longs to be gracious to us. We don't have to be stuck in sin, its consequences, or judgments of others. I don't know about you, but when I find out the Lord *longs* to give me something, I'm going to accept it eagerly with arms open wide.

Psalm 111 is a psalm of praise that lists just some of the ways God is gracious to us. Verses 1–4 extol the Lord for his works, ending by saying, "the Lord is gracious and compassionate." Verses 5–9 build on this sentence by giving support through examples, and it is listed below. Note all the ways it points out God's compassion and grace in relation to us.

He provides food for those who fear him; he remembers his covenant forever. He has shown his people the power of his works, giving them the lands of other nations. The works of his hands are faithful and just; all his precepts are trustworthy. They are established for ever and ever, enacted in faithfulness and uprightness. He provided redemption for his people; he ordained his covenant forever—holy and awesome is his name.

Our God is a gracious God indeed.

Have you experienced a work of the Lord on a personal level? When Cory and I were young parents, I was a stay-at-home mom. Money was tight, but we were thankful we could live on his salary. As you may know, life with two small kids can be joyous but tiring. One day, the kids and I were gearing up for their once-a-week Mother's Day Out Program. Cory hadn't left for work yet that morning, which was out of the norm, but he was a huge help getting the kids ready and buckling them up in our minivan. We kissed our goodbyes, shut the van doors, opened the garage, and started the *VeggieTales* songs. I then backed straight into Cory's truck.

Yes. I managed to wreck *both* of our vehicles at the same time.

You know how life with small kids can be distracting? Let's just say this wasn't the first incident with our poor minivan. I may or may not have also taken out a very innocent mailbox a few months earlier while trying to catch a falling sippy cup. We also had been dealing with some medical issues, and money was tight. Really tight. We had to decide if we would pay our tithe that month or have enough money to cover the bills.

We decided that God was always faithful to us, so we needed to be faithful to him. We wrote our tithe check and put it in the offering plate that Sunday. That very same day a man in the church we didn't know well came up to Cory and gave him an envelope. All he said was, "The Lord told me to give this to you," and then turned and walked away.

Cory didn't know what it was and went back into his office. He opened the envelope and, very emotionally, came to me. I was teaching a college class at the time, and Cory stuck his head in and told me he needed to show me something. I stepped out so we could talk, and he showed me the check. It was the exact amount we needed to cover our bills. We wept right there in the church parking lot while the Florida sun warmed us with God's grace.

What emotions come to the surface for you when you personalize how God has given grace to you? Do you have a grace story? Your story might not involve a gift or check but a word of encouragement. Maybe it was a neighbor helping out or receiving good news instead of bad news. When we look for God's grace, it can be seen in all sorts of places. We need to look for God's grace and understand it when we experience it.

Grace understood brings humility to our actions and allows us to marvel at the perfection of our Savior. Grace is beautiful because it meets us where we are, filth and all. It is completely unearned. Do you think we deserved that check? No. But God is the giver of all things good. Grace is a delicious concoction of love and mercy and kindness, and it brings joy and life to those who accept it. There is so much freedom in knowing we are not worthy of a relationship with our Creator but that it is freely offered to us through Christ. Titus 2:11 tells us, "For the grace of God has appeared that offers salvation to all people." And Ephesians 2:8 tells us, "For it is by grace you have been saved, through faith—and this is not from yourselves, it is the gift of God."

The Hebrew word for grace comes from the root word *chanan*, which means "to bend down to." [34] The cultural definition from biblical times is the concept of a loving parent bending down over a hurting child, like the good Samaritan helping the Israelite get back to health. Grace is God loving us on our level, helping us navigate the world around us. Grace is God, in his holiness, relating to his children.

Grace is similar to holiness because both are a picture of someone reaching in lovingly to help. God in his holiness is above and beyond us yet chooses to reach into our lives to interact with us out of his love. God in his grace bends down and loves us where we are, warts and all. His grace for us is not something we deserve because of our sin. God's grace comes out of the very character of God himself.

Grace can also be defined as undeserved favor. [35] To make it easy to understand, God's grace is God saying, "I love you *anyway*." We can feel the warmth of God's grace when he clothed Adam and Eve. We see it when scales dropped from Saul/Paul's eyes. We hear it in the crackle and pop of the charcoal fire at Peter's reinstatement. We taste it in the broiled fish when Jesus first appeared to the disciples after his resurrection.

Grace is God saying I love you despite…

What you've thought,
what you've said,
what you did,
who you were.

God's grace is free. It is everlasting. God's countenance overflows with compassion and mercy. It's just who he is. God loves us where we are and desires for us to be more like him every day. We can't earn grace because grace isn't about the one to whom it is given. Grace is all about the giver. Grace is all about God.

And remember what my buddy Spurge said… you are *way* worse than you even realize. Yet, God loves you *anyway*.

Chapter Questions

What is the Hebrew concept of grace?

How have you experienced this in your own life?

How does this compare to holiness?

Chapter Thirteen

SHINING, BLINDING GRACE

You guys, I love kayaking. Paddling lazily under the sun surrounded by God's creation, hearing the gentle rustling breeze in the trees and feeling the warmth of the sun on my face… it's perfection.

But it's only perfection when you've got all your gear. Without sunglasses, you'll have a headache in thirty minutes or less, easy. Without sunglasses, you don't have just one sun to contend with but two because the water's reflection doubles the sun's brightness. And when the water ripples, without sunglasses, those beautiful, peaceful sparkles become horrendous, multiple blinding lasers of death that attack your eyes and melt your brain. The water magnifies the glare of the sun, and lack of eye protection can take you from pleasure to pain in a hot minute. Knowing this, David Jeremiah must be a kayaker, or at least an outdoorsman, because he describes grace perfectly. He said, "Trying to comprehend grace in whole is like staring directly into one thousand suns."[36]

Amen, Dave, it can't be done.

So, let's put on our sunglasses and focus on some highlights as we springboard off the last chapter. Now that we have separated any confusion between grace and mercy, let's continue to define grace. Then we are going to examine how we respond to it and, finally, study how we should offer it to others. Those unique areas of grace need to be understood on a cellular level if our desire is to love others the way God loves us.

In the last chapter, we learned that the Hebrew definition of grace comes from the picture of God bending down to help his children.

This Hebrew concept of grace is all over the Old Testament. The first occurrence is in Genesis 6:8, when Noah found favor in the eyes of the Lord. It is seen when God delivered his people from Egypt, how he provided for them in the wilderness, when he formed an everlasting covenant with them, and his continued forgiveness even through their rebellion and, ultimately, bringing them into the Holy Land. We see grace in the stories of Joseph, Esther, and Samson. The concept of grace shines in the psalms and sparkles in Proverbs.

The Greek word used for grace in the New Testament is *charis*. Charis means "that which affords joy, pleasure, delight, sweetness, and charm."[37] It's where we get our word *charisma*. Charis eventually evolved in Greek to mean an actual gift, a literal offering of love and kindness to its recipient. God's gift of grace is God loving us where we are, no matter what we've done. It is more than forgiveness because we find an aspect of acceptance of us exactly as we are and loving us anyway. It is a delight, a pleasure that brings great joy, simply because our sins and faults are overlooked. Grace means we are loved purely and completely by our Creator.

The evidence of God's grace is personified in Jesus. There are all kinds of examples where he lived out the "I love you anyway" attitude: He ate with Zacchaeus; he gave Peter some fish. He helped the blind to see, touched the lepers, he listened to the hurting, and he drank water with a woman at a well.

On a personal level, can you think of examples when Jesus loved *you* anyway? To really get a picture of this, write some words on the outside of this page that only you and the Lord will understand, or on a piece of paper if you are reading on an ebook. Write words that symbolize times when you needed and experienced God's grace because your life at the time was less than stellar.

Some people out there—and I hope this isn't you—think what they have done is so bad, so evil, and so foul that God could never "love them anyway" because of their thoughts or actions. Those people are convinced they are eternally cut off from him no matter how hard they pray or lean into his will. Friend, read this closely. When you repent and run to God asking for his grace and forgiveness, he gives it.

Every.
Single.
Time.

Second Corinthians 12:9 says, "My grace is sufficient for you, for my power is made perfect in weakness." When *your* beautiful face is tearstained, *your* heart is shattered, and *you* are too weak to stand, God's grace is enough. He is enough. Run to him, cling to him, tell him everything because he is there for you. His power is there even when you have none. And that grace? It is sufficient for you.

Webster's Dictionary 1828 defines the word *sufficient* as "enough; equal to the end proposed."[38] In the above sentence, mark out the word *sufficient* and write above it the word *enough*. If something is enough, it is exactly what you need. A perfect fit for what is required. But here's even more good news about grace...

In 2 Chronicles 30:9 it says, "He will not turn his face from you if you return to him." I love that picture. When you look to him, he stares straight back at you, into your heart, your soul, your need. When you are hurting, draw close to your Father; he can and will meet your need.

There was a county judge who stared into the face of many a hurting child in the one-stoplight town of Wewahitchka, Florida. Judge David

Taunton was continually burdened when he saw minors having to deal with the fallout of decisions that were not their own. David's father had a dream of opening a children's home in the area, but having thirteen kids, he was never able to do so. David felt led to fulfill his father's dream. People in town were aware of his desires, and one woman was bold enough to get it going.

It all started over thirty-five years ago when David and his wife, Abigail, were asked by a woman with a pregnant teen if they would adopt the baby. They said yes and named him Adam because they knew he would be the first of many. Now, there have been over 300 children who have been under their care, all because they wanted to bend down into the hurting and love on these children. David and Abigail are wonderful examples of living lives of grace.

David passed away a year ago but was never seen without a smile on his face and a child close by. Those children were his home, his family. David's desire wasn't just to help children from far away but to look closely into their lives and love them where they were. Abigail is still in charge, and when I spoke with her, she was driving to a volleyball game ten hours away with one of her daughters. Not only did David then and Abigail now live lives of grace, they drew close to those who needed them.[39]

God is always waiting for us to draw close to him because he knows we need him. God created us to be in a relationship with him, but he will not force himself on anyone. His love is so valuable; we have the opportunity to choose it or reject it. When we choose him, he will not reject us… ever. To see this more clearly, draw a square around the word *not* in the 2 Chronicles verse above. Now, draw a circle around the word *if*. All we have to do to see his face is turn to him. That's it.

Hebrews 4:16 says, "Let us then approach God's throne of grace with confidence, so that we may receive mercy and find grace to help us in our time of need." Did you catch that? We are to approach the Lord's throne with confidence. Why? Because we can receive mercy and find grace to help us.

> We can receive mercy.
> We can find grace.

Remember, God gives us grace because of who he is, not who we are. He offers his grace in relationship, and in relationship is how we must receive it. We can be confident when we approach him because he has a throne of grace. Flip back a few pages to the symbols or letters you jotted down on the outside of your page. They symbolized when you needed God's grace. Now, over each one, draw a cross, and make your marks heavy and dark. As you do so, thank the Lord for covering you with his grace. Remember that after we fall down, once we reach up to him with a spirit of brokenness and repentance, his grace will be extended. God through his grace will lift us up and steady us on our feet. And he will do that *every* single time.

Close out this chapter by kneeling at the throne of grace. Have a conversation with the Lord, praising him for who he is, and receive what you need from him. His grace is enough.

Chapter Questions

What does the phrase "My grace is sufficient for you" mean to you? How can you apply it to your life?

Chapter Fourteen

CHEAP GRACE

I don't know about you, but the gift of God's grace humbles me to my knees. This morning I was talking to Cory about grace—over eggs and sausage no less—and getting his opinion on this chapter. As we were digging deep into breakfast and the idea of grace, I just started crying. I was overwhelmed with the Lord's love and acceptance of me, warts and all. Our God is so full of love, forgiveness, mercy, and… well, grace.

What we have been given is massive and eternal and something our human hearts and brains cannot comprehend. If we as Christians can begin to understand the grace we have been given, and respond to it appropriately, the world will be different. *We* will be different. However, instead of being in awe of God's constant provision of grace for me, I sometimes forget his grace is there. Or worse, I am aware of his grace, but take it for granted.

Have you ever done something with the thought, "It's better to ask forgiveness than permission?" My bet is you were trying to get away with something! That attitude is a great example of taking grace for granted. If we know we are going to have to ask for forgiveness for an action, then we probably shouldn't be doing it in the first place.

Every relationship has a give and take, and ours with the Lord is no different. We need to be conscious of how we *respond* to his grace.

Do we cherish it?
Demand it?
Assume it?
Ignore it?

How we interact with grace can draw us closer to or push us further away from understanding the character of God himself. In the last chapter, we focused on receiving grace. Today, we will study how we respond to it in our hearts.

Romans 6:14–16 says the following:

For sin shall no longer be your master, because you are not under the law, but under grace. What then? Shall we sin because we are not under law but under grace? By no means! Don't you know that when you offer yourselves to someone as obedient as slaves, you are slaves to the one you obey— whether you are slaves to sin, which leads to death, or to obedience, which leads to righteousness?

As Christians, we live under grace. We have a God who bends down to help us every day. To live under grace means we live under the protection of the Lord. He is your Father, and you are his child.

When I was four years old, my brother was fourteen. He played on his middle school football team, and my family never missed a game. Since it wasn't a varsity sport, there weren't formalities like a stadium or stands or cheerleaders. It was on the practice field at the high school with nothing separating the fans from the boys. Families and friends would stand on the sidelines and cheer the team, hopefully to victory.

Being a pre-kindergartener, I had other interests than football. I would bring crayons or dolls or do cartwheels and dance numbers while the game raged on. One afternoon, while I was twirling to the music in my head, a ball was thrown out of bounds. It was a long pass, unexpected, and honestly a pretty good throw. Everyone watching stepped back in an amoeba-like fashion. I, however, wasn't paying a lick of attention. I remember hearing a lady's panic-filled voice saying, "Someone get that little girl!" and then there was blackness.

I literally was sidelined by a fully clad receiver who was dutifully looking back for the ball. My hip had been dislocated. You know what my dad did? He ran over as fast as he could, bent down, picked me up off the ground, and carried me to the car. I was hurt, but my dad was there. He and mom talked to me the whole time we headed for the hospital, and they kept me as calm as possible. I never felt alone because I knew they were with me. I was under their grace and under their care.

The Greek word for "under" used in the Romans 6:14–16 verses we read earlier is *hupo*. It's a preposition referring to being under the authority of someone or something else.[40] To live under grace means we live under the authority, the power, the control of grace.

Those verses point out that we can be enslaved to sin or enslaved to obedience. It's not a pick and choose kind of deal, although the world would love for us to think we can be obedient in some areas and sinful in others and be okay with how we live our lives. Christian living is not based on a law of averages.

The difference between sin and obedience is staggering. If we are enslaved to sin, that life will lead to death. But if we choose to enslave ourselves to obedience, it will lead to righteousness. To make it super easy to understand, it looks like this:

- Sin = death
- Obedience = righteousness

When we choose to live under grace, we are committing to serve, to be enslaved as Paul put it, to righteousness and obedience. It is important that we realize grace is free, but it deserves a proper response from us. Without a proper response, the beautiful grace of God given through Christ's death on the cross can be presumed and then, knowingly or unknowingly, ignored.

It may seem odd to look at the challenges we have of grace—because it is *grace*—but we need to eradicate any misconceptions that can trip us up. I want us to become painfully aware of any negative responses we have around grace so we can toss them out like rotten potatoes. We make God's grace flippant when we take it for granted. We should not approach him with a brazenness to our sin and order him to offer grace for something we have no intention of making right because we know he promises grace when we need it. We can't knowingly live opposite God's precepts and expect his grace to fall upon us. Sin gives way to death. Obedience gives way to righteousness.

One day, I was approached by a person I didn't know well. This person looked me up and down and led with, "You need to forgive me, but I'm not going to tell you what I did to you." I managed to stammer out a shocked, "Um… okay" because in the moment I thought that was the Christlike thing to do. This person then reiterated how I had to forgive them since I was a Christian, and although they felt bad about what they had done, they couldn't really fix it. Then they walked away. It was a dumping of sin at my feet, leaving me standing in the mess wondering what was so vile that this person demanded forgiveness but could not own or admit the wrong.

In my shock, I reinforced an idea that weakens the fiber of grace. That person presumed absolution from guilt and grace was taken for granted. I accepted an "apology" offered without brokenness, without responsibility, without humility, sorrow, or really, even kindness. It was a self-serving request made without any thought of how that wrong affected me. That person made grace about themselves, the receiver, and not about the giver. Friends, we cannot do that to Jesus, who died for us.

German theologian Dietrich Bonhoeffer has outlined two ways we respond to God's grace. The first way is by treating grace as unimportant, something that is assumed and accepted because we think God's grace is all about us. This grace, and thus our relationship with Christ, is not cherished because it does not require any response except acceptance. It is presumptuous, arrogant, and entitled. It is grace where we keep living happily in our sin.

Bonhoeffer puts it like this: "Cheap grace is the preaching of forgiveness without requiring repentance, baptism without church discipline, communion without confession, absolution without personal confession. Cheap grace is grace without discipleship, grace without the cross, grace without Jesus Christ, living and incarnate."[41]

Cheap grace allows people to wallow in their sin assuming God's love for *us* is God's love for our *sin*. It is living on our terms rather than how the Bible tells us to live, and it completely misses the purpose of the gift of grace. Cheap grace is convenient Christianity. Hoard forgiveness for yourself and ignore the responsibilities of growing in your faith. Demand forgiveness, mercy, grace, and love from others, but you can stay as hardhearted, hateful, jealous, and selfish as you want.

The apostle Paul makes a great point when he asked in Romans 6:1, "Shall we go on sinning so that grace may increase?" Paul is pretty adamant in his response when he answers his own question with a "By no means!" He points out that we have died to sin and wonders why we would want to live in it any longer (Romans 6:2).

Titus 2:11–12 builds on this thought. It says, "For the grace of God has appeared that offers salvation to all people. It teaches us to say 'No' to ungodliness and worldly passions, and to live self-controlled, upright and godly lives in this present age."

Jesus, God's grace personified, conquered sin and death on the cross and offers us salvation from our sin. Because of his sacrifice, we should say no to ungodly things and strive to live in obedience as best we can. Jesus paid for our sin in full; he redeemed us. To ignore that fact and purposefully live in sin shows how we value his sacrifice.

Titus 2:14 goes on to explain that Jesus redeemed us so he could purify our hearts. The Greek word for redeem in this verse is the verb *lutroó* and means "to be set free by paying the full price; to restore something back into the possession of its rightful owner; rescue from the power of an alien possessor."[42]

It's not okay to live in cheap grace. We have been redeemed, traded in, restored. Living in cheap grace keeps our spirit shallow, unchallenged, and unchanged. It ignores and fights against spiritual growth. But Bonhoeffer talked about another kind of grace—what grace truly is—and we will continue that in the next chapter.

To really take grace seriously in your life, stop and ask the Lord to show you areas where you have cheapened his grace. Ask him for help to change. Invite his spirit to mold you. Cheap grace, because it isn't grace at all, is meaningless. Costly grace, however, is priceless.

Chapter Questions

What is cheap grace? How can we be careful not to take grace for granted in our lives?

Chapter Fifteen

COSTLY GRACE

I f your only exposure to Dietrich Bonhoeffer is his concept of cheap grace, I urge you to check out his biography. It's not short, but man, is it a good read. The title alone is fantastic: *Bonhoeffer: Pastor, Martyr, Prophet, Spy.* And yes, he really was *that* cool. I read his book *The Cost of Discipleship* while in college, and it caused a pivotal change in my spiritual life. It is where he discusses cheap grace and is what I referenced in the last chapter. Cheap grace is assumed, uncherished, and entitled. Now we are going to dig into the other type of grace he identified. Real grace. True grace. Grace that is greater than all our sin.

Bonhoeffer states the second way we can react to grace is through costly grace. Costly grace is empathetic to the cross of Christ. It is something we understand deeply and respond to appropriately. Costly grace is grace understood and has us responding to God in total obedience. The driving force of costly grace is a love relationship with our Father and the desire to live a life worthy of him.

Costly grace is aware of 1 Peter 1:18–19 (NLT): "For you know that God paid a ransom to save you from the empty life you inherited from your ancestors. And it was not paid with mere gold or silver, which lose their value. It was the precious blood of Christ, the sinless, spotless Lamb of God."

The currency the Lord used to save us from an empty life was the life-blood of his very own, very perfect, son. Our life has meaning because of Christ. Our life has purpose because of Christ. Understanding the grace of God in our lives keeps us full of thankfulness, humility, and love for our savior. So, to contrast and compare...

- Cheap grace = empty lives
- Costly grace = full lives

Cheap grace keeps our lives empty. Costly grace takes into account that God's grace came with a price—the life of his son. The value of experiencing costly grace fills us up beyond measure. When we choose to accept grace with the proper attitude, we know it costs something of us as well. Costly grace calls us to live a holy life. In 2 Timothy 1:9 it says, "He has saved us and called us to a holy life—not because of anything we have done but because of his own purpose and grace. This grace was given us in Christ Jesus before the beginning of time..."

To be clear, costly grace is not implying we are saved by works. It is grace valued and understood. Costly grace shows we cherish the gift of eternal life Christ gave us through the cross. It shows we are broken by our sin and desire to be faithful, not to earn salvation but to put Jesus's sacrifice at the place of utmost importance in our lives.

Bonhoeffer describes costly grace as "the gospel which must be sought again and again, the gift which must be asked for, the door at which a man must knock. Such grace is costly because it calls us to follow, and it is grace because it calls us to follow Jesus Christ. It is costly because it costs a man his life, and it is grace because it gives a man the only true life. It is costly because it condemns sin, and grace because it justifies the sinner. Above all, it is costly because it cost God the life of his Son: 'Ye were bought at a price,' and what has cost God much cannot be cheap for us."[43]

When we respond to God's grace, we must do so humbly, realizing it is out of God's character that he chose to offer his son. We should never view Jesus's death on the cross through entitlement but through the attitude of humility and thankfulness. Responding to God's grace means we begin to live a grace-filled life toward ourselves and others.

Remember how Paul told us in 2 Corinthians that God's grace is sufficient and enough for us?

To recap, when something is "enough," it means we have exactly what we need. We aren't wanting for anything. It is the perfect amount. When we understand and act on the belief that God's kindness, love, and unmerited favor are enough for us, we don't feel the need to look for validation elsewhere. Our need for significance is already filled by our most important relationship, the one with our Creator. We don't have to look to others, or to our successes, to find our confidence. A grace-filled life begins with the understanding that we are full of the grace that God has provided for us.

Once we understand God's grace, we must extend grace the same way it has been extended to us. For example, picture your life as a fountain but not a backyard trickle-and-bubble kind of thing. Think massive.

There is a fountain at the Palace of Versailles called the Latona Fountain, and it is considered one of the most beautiful in the world. It has three tiers and four pools and is made of gilded metal and marble. It is in the middle of the royal grounds with flowers and bushes and a fantastic view of the palace behind it. It's impossible to stand close to that fountain and not get wet. And who would want to? Isn't part of the experience to not only see its breathtaking beauty but to feel the coolness and wetness of the water? So much refreshment pours out of it; it's going to get on everyone around it. It got on me when I was there. And I *loved* it.

When grace flows freely into our lives, it overflows into our relationships, sometimes consciously and many times unconsciously. Grace understood means that grace is offered to others naturally. It flows out of us the way the water flows out of the Latona Fountain, with a gentle force that gets all over everyone around you. Grace shared is Christ manifesting himself in us through the Holy Spirit. It was Philip Yancey who wrote, "We respond to healing grace by giving it away."[44] You can tell a lot about someone's understanding of the grace they have received by the grace they give to others.

Second Corinthians 8:1–10 is a beautiful encouragement showing us how we should act in grace. This passage is talking about generosity in sharing the grace given, both tangible and intangible. I want us to focus on 2 Corinthians 8:7, which I've listed below:

But since you excel in everything—in faith, in speech, in knowledge, in complete earnestness and in the love we have kindled in you—see that you also excel in this grace of giving.

Did you catch what we are supposed to excel in?

- Faith
- Speech
- Knowledge
- Earnestness
- Love
- Grace of giving

Let grace abound in all your relationships. Don't hold back, in any area, with anyone. If you must, pray for God's strength, power, and grace until you can offer it the same way God has offered it to you. We know what grace is. We know we must cherish it. We know we must respond to it, and we know we must let it flow out of us if we wish to be like Christ. Strive toward this. Seek it. Pray for it. The more natural it becomes, I am convinced, the more joyful we will be.

Chapter Questions

What is costly grace? How can we live this out in our lives?

Chapter Sixteen

DEFINING THE GOSPEL

n this chapter, we are going to traverse back thousands of years into the etymology of the word *gospel*. (Hint: It's not Greek.) I get it. It sounds dry but wait for it. I promise interesting stuff is ahead! When we are aware of what it meant in biblical times, we can be empowered and encouraged when we talk about it. Stopping at the definition of gospel as "good news" is like saying strawberry shortcake is made up of strawberries, whipped cream, and shortcake. That *is* a true statement, but break it down further, and the shortcake ingredients emerge—flour, sugar, butter, baking soda, and salt. My desire is for you to comprehend the word *gospel* in its exciting, individual parts.

Merriam-Webster defines the word *gospel* one way as "the message concerning Christ, the kingdom of God, and salvation."[45] And that is a great start. But let's get away from our modern viewpoint, travel through the Greco-Roman culture, and begin in the Hebrew world in the time of King David, which puts us about one thousand years before Christ.

The word is *bisar*.

Originally, it was military lingo. People longed to hear *bisar* when their loved ones, friends, and neighbors were at war with their enemies. It meant "to proclaim good news from battle." If the Israelites were successful in a conflict, a messenger was sent with a positive declaration back to the city gates, or to the palace, or both.[46] We see it clearly in 2 Samuel 4:8–10. Read those verses now. When you see the words "good news," the word is a form of *bisar*. To put this into practice, read the 2 Samuel verses again, replacing "good news" with "victory."

Bisar was to proclaim victory because the battle had been won. The people were free from being lorded over by another group and were still under their God and king. The messenger thought he was bringing victory to David, but David knew his victory of becoming king over all of Israel would only come from the Lord.

The Israelites believed God was actively involved in every area of their lives, including battles and wars, so the word bisar began to take on a religious meaning. The Israelites were God's people, and when they experienced victory, it was understood that God was victorious too. The word bisar started to shift from having the sole meaning of a victory in battle to God having victory over his and his people's enemies.[47]

We see this mindset transform even further when it began to be used on a personal level. The thought was if bisar was celebrated with the Israelites victories, it also should be celebrated when God delivered them from personal issues.

In Isaiah 52:7, we see the full impact and development of this theological concept. Bisar was most often used to describe deliverance and salvation that would come through the promised Messiah.[48] Here is Isaiah 52:7 in the New Living Translation:

How beautiful on the mountains are the feet of the messenger who brings good news, the good news of peace and salvation, the news that the God of Israel reigns!

If you don't mind writing in your book, to get a better idea of bisar in its original sense, mark out the words "good news" in the verse above and instead write the word "victory." Now read it again.

How amazing is *that*?

Just to complete the etymology, let's move from Hebrew to Greek. Once Rome conquered most of the known world, including areas where the Israelites lived, Greek became the common language that crossed cultural barriers in the empire. The Greek word *euangelizesthai* was similar to bisar, as it was used to proclaim a win in battle. By New Testament times, the meaning changed slightly and simply meant "to proclaim." The word morphed again and changed to *euangelion* (where we get our word *evangelism*). English replaced the Greek with *godspell*, which means "the story about a god," and was used with the good news of Christ. It then was shortened to our word *gospel*, which became associated with the one true God and his Son, Jesus Christ.[49]

The word *gospel* is talking about the victory we have in Christ. When we share the gospel with someone, we are sharing the victory Christ has in our lives over sin and death. (1 Corinthians 15:57) It really is that simple!

Jesus is our victor. He is also our overcomer. John 16:33 says, "I have told you these things, so that in me you may have peace. In this world you will have trouble. But take heart! I have overcome the world."

The Greek word used here is nikaó and means "to conquer, prevail; overcome; to carry off the victory, come off victorious."[50] A form of this word is *nike*—like the brand name—and means victory. The verb actually implies a battle.[51]

This world *is* a battle for our souls, between good and evil, life and death, truth and lies, freedom and bondage. The battle is between the God of the Universe and the ultimate liar, who wants to keep you from the truth of God. Our victory is only found in Christ.

Let's look at the following verses to understand this concept further. First John 5:4–5 (NLT) reads:

For every child of God defeats this evil world, and we achieve this victory through our faith. And who can win this battle against the world? Only those who believe that Jesus is the Son of God.

To really make this pop, go ahead and circle the word *only* in the paragraph above. Now underline the sentence before it. Only those who believe in Jesus have the victory over sin and death. We can't be victorious by ourselves. It is found in Christ. He is our victor. He is our savior. He is who we are to proclaim to anyone and everyone who will listen.

The gospel is important for us to share. Second Timothy 1:8 tells us we should not be ashamed to tell others about the Lord. So, what keeps us from telling others about the saving grace of Jesus?

- Is it because societal norms tell us we shouldn't?
- Is it because we are afraid of what others will think?
- Is it because we think we can't do it correctly?

Let me tell you about Katie. Katie spreads the gospel the way wild-flowers spread in the sun. I met Katie when she was a college student involved in our collegiate ministry. She had not been raised in church, but first visited ours to see her sister get baptized. Katie had never heard the good news of Christ before, and she accepted Jesus into her heart a few short weeks after visiting. Her life was forever changed, and over the next few weeks, she did a 180-degree turn in how she lived her life.

Katie went from partier to prayer in a hot minute, all the while telling people about the Lord. She would walk up to people she didn't know on campus and befriend them just so she could tell them about Christ. She was friendly and kind and bold in the Lord, and so earnest about her newfound love of Jesus that her passion made people want to listen to what she had to say. Katie prayed for the Lord to put someone in her path each week with whom she could share Jesus, and in that first semester of her new life in the Lord, she led one or more people to Jesus *each week*!

Katie didn't feel intimidated or embarrassed or awkward. She was just really excited about what God had done in her life and wanted others to have that too. Katie didn't want anyone to go to hell. She never over-thought how to share the gospel, or debated why she should share, or waited until she was trained with a twelve-step program. She shared the victory in her life simply by telling her story, loving others, and being excited about Jesus.

Katie knew that the gospel is simple to explain. It isn't hard or uncomfortable to discuss. Those, my friend, are lies to keep you from living out your victory in Christ. Think about it. Who doesn't love a story where the good guy wins?

The gospel is this: All of us have sinned, and that sin separates us from God. Jesus defeated sin when he died on the cross and came back to life. When we ask Jesus to conquer the sin in our lives, he will. He comes into our heart through our faith in him and promises he will be with us forever. And because our faith is real, we live how he says we should live—because living any other way would be second best.

Do you know someone who needs the victory of Jesus in their lives? Why not add them to your prayer list and begin lifting up their hearts to God daily. Ask the Lord for boldness to share the win in your own life and opportunities for you to step into conversation.

Let the gospel define your own life as well. If you have asked Jesus into your heart, he has won the victory over sin and death in your life. Don't get pulled back into a life of defeat, sadness, and despair. His victory should define not only you but how you see the world. He is a victor, and you are on his team. Go out and live like it!

Chapter Question

How can the victory found in Christ have a deeper effect on your everyday relationships?

Chapter Seventeen

SALVATION

A few years ago, I attempted to learn French. We were headed to Paris, and I deeply desired to talk to people without any barriers. I don't pick up on languages easily, so this was a long, hard fight. When our time of departure came, the popular app I had been using told me I'd achieved the high fluency rate of... 21 percent. If you need to understand one out of every five words, I'm your girl!

Being released into the Parisian wild, we went to a place called Bistrot Paul Bert (pronounced "Bear"), which served one of the best meals I've ever had in my life. At Paul Bert, I am confident they cook food the way God intends it to be eaten. Months earlier I had called and made our reservations, *en français*, but they knew I was *une Américaine* by my butchered accent. Being the group's only interpreter, my nerves were jumping out of my skin. As soon as our waiter came to the table, I chickened out and quickly used my French to ask for an English menu!

The waiter got the funniest look on his face and made a grand gesture to the massive chalkboard sign right beside our table. He waved his arm while saying perfectly in *my* native tongue, "It eeezz in English!" We all laughed and relaxed, knowing we could be understood. The point was, they knew I could converse in French—sort of—and they had made preparations so we all (waitstaff included) would be comfortable during the meal.

Look, friends, I don't want you to *sort of* understand salvation the way I *sort of* understand French. My desire is for you to know the word's meaning so you will be confident when you share this concept with someone. I want you to apply salvation to your own life and live it out daily. The saying is true: Knowledge *is* power. As we define and discuss salvation, keep in mind how both your personal conversion experience and how growing in your faith has affected your life.

Acts 4:11–12 reads, "Jesus is the stone you builders rejected, which has become the cornerstone. Salvation is found in no one else, for there is no other name under heaven given to mankind by which we must be saved."

The Greek word used for salvation here is *soteria*, which means deliverance or salvation.[52] This word soteria can also be used to refer to someone's welfare, preservation, prosperity, and safety in their life. Soteria comes from the root word *sozo*, which means to save or rescue.[53] Knowing that, I want to reiterate what it says above but also plug in some definitions of words that are a little more common to help us apply this gift to our lives.

- My *deliverance* is found in no one else.
- My *welfare* is found in no one else.
- My *preservation* is found in no one else.
- My *prosperity* is found in no one else.
- My *safety* is found in no one else.

The salvation Christ offers us is safety from the evil one, as well as preservation from death and destruction. Salvation gives us a prosperous spiritual life through a relationship with Jesus.

In Hebrew, the word used for salvation is *yasa* and means "to rescue, to deliver, and to bring to safety."[54] There is a play on words in Hebrew paralleling Jesus and salvation, and let me tell you, the biblical authors *loved* a good play on words. Jesus's Hebrew name was Yeshu'a. His name is derived from the verb version *yasha* (from yasa), which points to what Jesus was to fulfill here on earth. In Matthew 1:21, an angel of the Lord appeared to Joseph in a dream. The angel would have said in native Hebrew, "You are to name him Yeshu'a, because he will yasha people from their sins."[55]

Another play on words to show that Jesus offers salvation to us is found in Isaiah 11:1, "A shoot will come up from the stump of Jesse; from his roots a Branch will bear fruit." Notice how the word "Branch" is capitalized? The word used is *netzer*, and it means a sprout or shoot. Jesus was from the town of Nazareth (in Hebrew "Natzeret"), so our salvation comes from a Netzer from Natzeret.[56] It is the prophecy that Matthew 2:23 refers to when he says, "He will be called a Nazarene."

It is not uncommon to see netzers shooting off the stumps of olive trees found anywhere in Israel. If left untouched, they will grow into part of the tree. A cut netzer can be seen on the front cover of this book. I like this image for us, because when we are Deeply Defined, we can be an offshoot of the father as we strive to have the same attributes as Christ.

In the Old Testament, salvation and deliverance are usually thought of as a physical thing (think of the exodus from Egypt), but in the New Testament, it morphs into something physical while keeping and expanding on its spiritual significance. The Greek word for salvation, *soteria*, brings with it "health, well-being, and healing."[57]

To cover salvation on the most basic level, we can look to Romans 10:9–10. That verse clearly states if we confess with our mouths that Jesus is Lord and believe in our hearts that he was raised from the dead, *we will be saved!*

When we believe Jesus is the Son of God who died and rose again, we are made right with God. When we confess, we are saved from our sin. Salvation, like grace, cannot be earned. It is a gift we accept through faith in Jesus Christ.

The best tangible gift I've ever received was from my husband, and to the outsider, it looks like a plain chunk of wood. Before my parents moved out of the home I grew up in, they cut down a massive sassafras tree that had been right outside of my bedroom window. I'd loved that tree, with its differing shaped leaves and the gorgeous colors it turned every fall, for as long as I could remember. That tree had been right outside my window throughout childish dreams, teenage heartbreaks, and bridal jitters. I'd sat under it with my children and had some amazing talks in the shade with my folks. Cory knew that tree was close to my heart, so he broke a piece off from the stump after the rest had been carted off for firewood. He kept that piece of wood in his truck for several years until my mom and dad moved.

The last day I walked through that house, I was a bit emotional but held it together until I got into the truck. Cory then handed me the piece of wood and told me what it was. I burst into tears for that thoughtful gift. Because of what Cory did, I have a part of that tree with me. Now, that chunk sits on a bookshelf in my living room, and I see it every day. That gift was given out of love. That gift connected to my heart.

The gift of salvation connects our hearts to the Lord. When we accept Jesus as our savior, the Holy Spirit comes and promises to never leave us or forsake us. It is the free gift of God in our lives because salvation cannot be earned.

It actually is *impossible* to earn salvation. It is a gift of grace given by our Creator to save us from our sins. We can't earn it through church attendance or by being a good person. It isn't based on people we know, where we come from, or our DNA. The Lord bends down and offers his hand to all, and when we respond by reaching up to him, he pulls us out of the pit. He has chosen to save us by plunging his hand into the muck and mire of our lives where we are the most sinful and dirty and lost and hopeless, where we are sinking and flailing and screaming for someone to care. He replaces hopelessness with hopefulness and despair with divine dealings. He offers healing and love and truth and a future through Jesus's death on the cross, burial, and resurrection.

We must knowingly *choose to respond* to God's offer of salvation in our lives.

That is the beginning of our salvation experience, our own *victory* in and through Jesus Christ. Once we have been introduced to the Son of God and accept him as Lord, Savior, and Friend, it is our responsibility to mature and experience him every day. When salvation is real, Jesus becomes an integral part of our lives. We praise him in our highs and run to him in our lows. We have the privilege of experiencing a valued relationship with him this very second.

Salvation in Christ means more than going to heaven when we die. It is for our current circumstance (2 Corinthians 6:2). We are saved *from* death in sin but also saved *for* life in Christ. If we miss out on experiencing the gift of salvation now, we miss out on all kinds of blessings the Lord desires for us to have.

To be super clear, our salvation experience isn't just our conversion experience. It is a daily relationship lived out in all of our challenges. It is redemption for our failures and celebration in our victories. Jesus came to save us from our sin, but he also came to save us from ourselves, our shame, our mistakes, our pride, and our pain. Jesus came to save every part of us in every situation. I hope today you will go and live out your salvation in joy and peace. I hope you will feel the presence of God around you. I hope you will shine the light of his love into the dark places of people's souls. Salvation is *now*. Embrace it!

Chapter Question

If you were going to share the gospel with someone, what would you say?

Chapter Eighteen

HEAR AND OBEY

As a kid, did you have *that* tree? You know the one. Perfect for climbing, for swinging, for jumping out of, basically channeling your young, compacted energy into monkey-dom. My tree was in the front yard, right beside the driveway. The branches were spread far enough apart so you could comfortably sit for hours in the shade with a Capri Sun in one hand and a friend just a few leaves away. The tree was full and verdant enough to be the perfect hiding spot when my friend's mom would come to take her home. We knew if we stayed long enough, our moms would get to talking, and if things were really in our favor, they'd go inside for a cup of coffee. But the test, the one where we held our breath, was when my friend's mom arrived and we were called.

"Kiiiiiiddddss????"
"Jaaaaaaa-neeeeeeyyyyy."

Sometimes we were obedient. They would call, we would come. I don't know if we were tired or just feeling particularly righteous on those days, but we'd respond immediately and climb down from our arborous sanctum. Other days, we would hold our breath. Hope they wouldn't know we were hiding in the tree. Sometimes it worked, and we'd get thirty extra minutes while the moms caffeinated to bank energy for the remainder of the day. Other times they'd march over to the tree, look up, and then... the question.

"Did you hear us calling?"

Of course, we did; they were thirty feet away. But were we always honest? Nope. You know the drill; I bet you said it to your mom too... "We didn't hear you! We didn't know you meant we *had* to come down. We thought you meant in a little while, not right *now*." And the defense continued until my friend pulled out and was on her way home. We knew if we said we had heard them then we would be admitting to disobedience.

Let me tell you, friends, in biblical times, hearing and then not doing wouldn't have had a chance. Culturally, that would have not been done. In both the Old and New Testaments, hearing and obeying were the *same thing*.

Deuteronomy 11:13 is written to the Hebrew people as God is telling them how they should live. The verse begins with, "So if you faithfully obey the commands I am giving you today..." But if you read this verse literally in Hebrew, which is how they would have heard it in biblical times, they would have read, "And it will be if hearing, you will hear..."

The Hebrew word used is *Shema*.[58]

You may have heard that word before. The Shema is the name of a Jewish prayer that in biblical times was said multiple times a day. It still is said by practicing Jews even in current times. It can be said at weddings and at funerals and is a basis for how the Jewish people relate to God. It is called the Shema because that is the first word in the verses taken from Deuteronomy 6:4, "Hear, O Israel: The Lord our God, the Lord alone."

So far, we see that shema can mean hear or obey because they are interchangeable in the culture in which it was written. Another example

of the word shema is found when the Israelites responded to Moses' recit-
ing of the covenant in Exodus 24:7. After Moses read the Book of the
Covenant to all the people, they responded to the reading by saying, "We
will do everything the Lord commanded; we will *obey*" (emphasis mine).

Again, the Hebrew reads differently than our English Bibles. It can
literally be translated, "All that God has said we will do, and we will
hear."[59] Shema means to listen, to hear, to obey. These words were one
and the same to the Hebraic reader, and should be seen as parallel in
meaning with us now. The best way for us to understand it, instead
of putting in one definition or the other for shema, is to use the word
shema itself.

> We will do what you say Lord, and we will shema.
> Don't you want that to be your prayer?

How does it change things when you understand hearing and obey
ing mean the same thing? To hear the Lord, yet not do what he is telling
you to do, is to be disobedient. You know how there are sins of commission and omission? Not doing something the Lord is telling you
to do is a sin because we are withholding our lives from his will. And,
if we know how God's Word says we are to live and choose not to do
them, that is disobedience as well. Biblical culture could tell us we aren't
hearing very well.

That's an eye opener, isn't it! The bottom line is when we hear what
God is telling us how we should act, when to love, and what to live for,
and we choose to follow our own path, we are not being obedient. Our
hearts are hard and not tuned in enough to hear him clearly. When we
hear from God, our natural inclination should be to respond to him.
Every. Single. Time. This response comes out of thankfulness, humility,
relationship, and love. The more we understand who he is, the deeper
our desire to respond to him immediately. The less we understand about

who God is, the less response we give. What we must not do is read God's Word, be aware of his will, and respond to him like I did to my mom from the tree…

> I didn't hear you, God.
> I didn't know you were calling me to do that.
> I thought you meant later on in my life, not right now.

Shema is hearing that brings immediate obedience. Delayed obedience is just disobedience in denial. From now on, when you read the word "hear" in the Bible, I want you also to think "obey." And when you see the word "obey," also know it means "hear." Knowing these two words are seen as the same, let's take this cultural knowledge into the New Testament.

The Greek word for hear (*akouo*) doesn't tell us much, except the root for "hear" is where we get our word acoustics.[60] Neat, but the Greek mindset had lost the concept of hearing = obeying. Luke 11:28 clearly states hearing and obeying go together, but he had to use two different words to do so. Luke was trying to get the Hebraic idea across that they are the same thing. The parable of the farmer scattering seed in Matthew 13:1–9 deals with the concept of shema. At the end of the parable, Jesus really wants the listeners to understand, so he literally says in Greek, "Whoever has ears, let them hear." Remember, Jesus came out of a Jewish culture. When he said this, he just wasn't urging his disciples to listen. His desire for them was to understand, then put the parable into practice.

Think that is a jump? James, the brother of Jesus, thought it too. We can see it in James 1:22–25:

> Do not merely listen to the word, and so deceive yourselves.
> Do what it says. Anyone who listens to the word but does

not do what it says is like someone who looks at his face in a mirror and, after looking at himself, goes away and immediately forgets what he looks like. But whoever looks intently into the perfect law that gives freedom and continues in it— not forgetting what they have heard, but doing it—they will be blessed in what they do.

Even though this is in the New Testament, we see the influence of shema. We can't just listen to God's Word; we must live it out. I like how James phrases it; we can't just look intently into God's Word; we must *continue* in it. Living out our faith is not a start-stop-start-stop kind of thing. We must strive for consistency simply out of our love for the Lord. We are not going to be perfect; we are going to mess up, but our mindset should be of obedience.

Obedience is simply knowing and doing what the Lord wants us to do. When we hear love your neighbor, avoid gossip, give to the needy, fight for justice, or offer mercy because God has been merciful to us, and we don't do those things, we are being disobedient. In our culture, that can be a hard pill to swallow. We like to explain disobedience away or make ourselves feel better with an "I'll do it later" attitude.

Step back a few paces and see it from a biblical viewpoint. Delayed obedience is disobedience. When God speaks, we need to hear, listen, and then respond. We respond when we hear of Jesus's death, burial, and resurrection. We respond when we hear God's will for our lives. We respond when we are available to listen… and then do what he says.

Ask the Lord what he wants you to hear from him in your life right now… what is he calling you to *do*? Remember, you were created for a reason and a purpose. Once you are aware of his voice, why wouldn't you want to *shema*?

Chapter Questions

What's the meaning of *shema*? How has the concept of hearing and obeying changed since biblical times?

Chapter Nineteen

BELIEF AND FAITH

F our years ago, my family moved into our current home. One reason we bought the house was for the land around it. Behind us, a river flows, surrounded by trees that are then surrounded by farmland. It is beautiful. We never know what animals are going to meander into our backyard. We have deer, opossums, raccoons, cardinals, blue jays, bunnies, skunks, squirrels, and to my dismay, an occasional snake, and then there's my favorite: turkeys. Friends, I can completely geek out over a good turkey.

I have a theory that turkeys and peacocks are distantly related. Think about it. Their bodies are the same, with tail feathers in the back that spread out when they are trying to impress other sexy beasts that could be turned on by such a thing. In my book, they are basically the same fundamentally. The Persian bird is just more colorful and flamboyant with better plumage. Now, I love a good turkey sandwich (made with store-bought turkey), but I can't swallow the thought of digesting peacock. Although they are similar, I must admit they are very different animals.

That's how I see the words *belief* and *faith*. They are close in meaning and are based on the same idea, but when defined in Hebrew, we can see a subtle nuance. When we focus on the differences of the words, we understand both more clearly.

A few chapters ago we learned about the good news, the victory Jesus has over sin and death. We learned we can share in that victory when we respond to Jesus by accepting the salvation that can only come from him. We learned that when we truly hear God's call on our life, obedience follows. In this chapter, we are taking all these concepts further and exploring the word… faith.

Romans 10:17 tells us that faith comes from hearing the gospel message, and we hear the message through the word of God. Paul then points out that not everyone who hears about Christ will accept him. He says that, although the people knew what God had said, they didn't truly hear, because they hadn't responded in obedient understanding. Their hearts were unmoved. In verse 21, Paul calls people with unmoved hearts disobedient and obstinate.

It is important to experience a faith that is more than a belief inside of us. Our faith must be lived out in our attitudes, words, and actions for it to be applied faith. It's not enough to have faith when it is convenient or when things are tough or when we want to feel good about ourselves in Sunday morning church. Applied faith is total surrender to what God says is best.

Total.

It is wisdom. Peace. Joy. It is loving our neighbor and forgiving others and being generous with our time, compliments, money, and opinions of others.

In the Old Testament, belief and faith stem from the same Hebraic root word but are seen as two slightly different things. One is a verb, the other a noun. The first time in the Bible we see the idea of belief is in Genesis 15:6. It says Abraham believed and it was credited to him as righteousness.

Again, we see the concept of responding. Just like hearing leads to obeying, believing leads to action. Righteousness is a big word with a simple meaning. It just means "to live out what God says is right." Righteousness is following God's laws, doing what his Word says, and keeping the spirit of how God tells us to live. In biblical times, righteousness described a person who contributed to the moral fiber of society. It meant having a proper attitude toward God and his ways.[61] We shouldn't say we believe or have faith in God and then not live it out. It's just not how it works.

We see faith stories all throughout the Bible. Shadrach, Meshach, and Abednego in the fire, Daniel in the lion's den, Esther before the king begging for the deliverance of her people. We see Peter walking on the water and going off on the Sanhedrin. If these people had talked about faith but not lived it out, God would not have been able to move in their lives like he did.

Because they believed in God, they lived out their faith.

A word used in Exodus for believe is a Hebrew root word, *aman*. It's a verb that means to confirm or support, to securely trust or rely upon, and it's where we get our word *amen*.[62] When we say amen to something, we are affirming that what has been stated is true and trustworthy. To get a mental picture, we can look at the concrete meaning of the word *aman*, as most Hebrew words have not only conceptual meanings but also define something physical. In 2 Kings 18:16, aman is used to mean support and is translated as the word *doorposts*.[63]

The Hebrew word for faith is the noun *emunah* (from the root *aman*). And man, oh man, is it a great word. It is first seen in this story found in Exodus 17:8–13:

The Amalekites came and attacked the Israelites at Rephidim. Moses said to Joshua, "Choose some of our men and go out to fight the Amalekites. Tomorrow I will stand on top of the hill with the staff of God in my hands." So Joshua fought the Amalekites as Moses had ordered, and Moses, Aaron and Hur went to the top of the hill. As long as Moses held up his hands, the Israelites were winning, but whenever he lowered his hands, the Amalekites were winning. When Moses' hands grew tired, they took a stone and put it under him and he sat on it. Aaron and Hur held his hands up—one on one side, one on the other—so that his hands remained steady till sunset. So, Joshua overcame the Amalekite army with the sword.

Did you see it? That's the right passage, but it is easy to miss. It's the first time in the Bible we see the Hebrew word for faith used in Scripture. The word is *emunah*, and it doesn't translate into one word in English. That's why the English word *faith* wasn't in the text you just read. This concept that we have translated to the word *faith* is broad and deep and beautiful. Emunah is used at the end when it says, "so that his hands *remained steady* till sunset."

Emunah means firmness, steadfast, fidelity.[64] Emunah is faithful and unmoving and remains steady and sure. Faith is a committed, consistent, ongoing relationship with our Creator. That is why it is said we are to *live out* our faith and not just keep it hidden in our hearts. How do we know this to be true? James 2:19 points out even the demons believe God is real. But would you say the demons are faithful to God?

Absolutely not.

They have rejected the King of the Universe and do everything they can to hinder his will in our lives. They will confirm there is a God but have no desire for a committed, ongoing relationship based in the truth that he is King, Lord, and Creator of all. The difference between the use of a verb and a noun in the usage of the root *aman* is notable because it personalizes the word.

For instance, the word *run* is a verb. But "runner" is a noun. "To speak" is a verb, while a "speaker" is a noun. To have belief means it produces something in your life, as with Abraham, whose deep relationship with God produced righteous living. To say you are a believer personifies the concept and changes it from something you do to someone you are. It is saying you are faithful to the Lord.

Faithfulness is a natural outpouring of our belief system. It is learning to be steadfast in your relationship with Jesus Christ and living out steadfast love to all. When we see ourselves as faithful, we do not view any part of who we are as outside of Christ. No area is untouched or hardened or ignored. At least it shouldn't be.

Is there an area of your life where you could be more faithful (steadfast) to God's ways? It could be to love and not hate, to be more generous, to forgive, or to offer mercy. It could be to worry less, to put your personal value in Christ, or to use the gifts you've been given for the Lord. I think when we constantly are introspective about our faith, it helps us grow. And when we grow, we come closer to being the person the Lord created us to be. When we are faithful, we reflect aspects of God.

Deuteronomy 32:3–4 says: "I will proclaim the name of the Lord. Oh, praise the greatness of our God! He is the Rock, his works are perfect, and all his ways are just. A faithful God who does no wrong, upright and just is he."

To make this verse hit home, let's use a more common definition for these churchy words. Right here in your book, in the above verse, mark through the word *faithful* and replace it with another word that emunah can be translated into, which is "steadfast." See how the idea of being steadfast also echoes the concept of God being a rock earlier in the verse?

Our God is an immoveable, faithful God. He is strong, sure, steadfast. We see a great description of faith in Hebrews 11:1. It says, "Now faith is confidence in what we hope for and assurance about what we do not see."

The Greek word used for faith in the above verse is *pistis* and means faith, trust, to believe.[65] Again, we see the idea of being sure and certain, steadfast, and true. Pistis is where we get our word *piston* (in cars), and learning what an automotive piston *does* helps us understand what pistis *is*. I encourage you to casually drop this knowledge into a conversation with your husband the next time he talks about cars. You will get serious brownie points, trust me.

A piston transfers force from the cylinder, where gasoline expands, to the crankshaft, which is what makes the car start. The gas expands in the cylinder, which forces the piston up until a release of pressure causes a small explosion, which brings the piston down again. It is an up-and-down movement caused by small explosions of power propelling the pistons along. Without the pistons, the car would not move. Without God's power moving in our lives, we would not move along and grow in our faith.

Now that we understand the Greek and Hebrew meanings of faith, we can expand our knowledge and seek how God wants us to live in the world around us. Why? Because unapplied faith isn't faith at all. Close out this chapter by asking the Lord how he wants his power to explode in your life and propel your faith forward into action. But be warned. When you ask, he will answer. And you won't be sitting on your couch for long.

Chapter Question

What do you think is the difference between belief and faith?

Chapter Twenty

SHOW OFF THAT FAITH

When I was in high school, our music program was arguably the best in the state. It was a behemoth force that overflowed with classes consisting of girls' choir, guys' choir, a mixed concert choir, and a smaller elite chamber ensemble. And can you believe the teacher had teenagers actually wanting to take a hard music theory class? It's true.

My sophomore year, greatness occurred. I made show choir, which basically meant I had arrived *in life*. It was a big deal to make the cut, and by achieving that goal my elation was thrust into the stratosphere. But it gets even better. The cast had *jackets*. Only those in the show could wear them. In the ultimate style of the day, they were a shiny, black satin-polyester blend with our "Brighter Touch of Orange" show logo stitched onto the back. The crowning glory was that I also made dancer, which was stitched right under my name on the left front pocket area. Listen, if I could have showered in that jacket, I would have.

I've never been prouder to don a piece of material in my life, and I couldn't wait to put it on every day. In my teenage understanding, it showed who I had become. I felt like it gave me a tribe, a people.

We need to realize the Lord has outfitted each of us, and we have been grafted into the tribe of the Lion of Judah. We are God's people. We don't have to arrive spiritually or make the cut to get our white robes. We simply have to accept the love and salvation offered through Christ. Ephesians 6 tells us to put on the armor of God. And for some reason, I feel like we aren't as excited about modeling it daily the way I was about my black satin-polyester prize. I think we take our armor for granted, or we don't understand it, or we get it out only when we feel we need it. The rest of the time, we just shove it into the back of our spiritual closet. But every believer has their armor, and we are to put it on every day. Ephesians 6:10–12 actually has a lot to say about this very topic:

> Finally, be strong in the Lord and in his mighty power. Put on the full armor of God, so that you can take your stand against the devil's schemes. For our struggle is not against flesh and blood, but against the rulers, against the authorities, against the powers of this dark world and against the spiritual forces of evil in the heavenly realms.

We do struggle every day, and it is not with the reality that we can see, touch, and feel. It is with the deeper reality of spiritual forces that want to keep you from being an effective soldier for Christ. Later in Ephesians 6 it lists off the armor of God, and one of the parts of that armor we are to put on is the shield of faith.

Just like the perfect purse pulls together an outfit, the shield of faith pulls together who we are in Christ. Our faith shields us from the arrows of the evil one. It helps us to be steadfast and sure in how we live, in who we are. The shields Paul is referring to aren't little yardstick-size things either. They are full-body size Roman shields used in the culture of the day. They are used as much for offense as they are defense. These shields covered everything from head to toe, keeping the warrior safe in combat. What do we do with this faith? Ephesians 2:8–9 tells us *we are saved by grace through faith.*

We are not saved by works, yet we respond in steadfastness to God's teachings by living out what we know to be true. There is no pressure to be perfect. News flash: I fail all the time. But God is there with his love, mercy, forgiveness, and grace to teach me and help me grow to become more like him. As 2 Corinthians 5:7 says, we live by faith, not by sight. When we are grounded and shielded by the Lord and his ways, life as we know it isn't as scary. It's not hopeless or overwhelming. We know God has a plan for us and that we are saved *for* something as well as *from* death. Not only does our faith shield us, but it also helps propel us forward.

We have many biblical examples of how God's people stayed steadfast. As a matter of fact, the first thirty-one verses of Hebrews 11 have "by faith" written twenty-one times. That is two out of every three verses, my friends! It lists tons of "famous" biblical characters who lived by faith. I'd say that qualifies as something to be noted.

It is easy for us to see when we have failed God and fallen in our faith. But it's important to realize that God has used you in many ways for his glory. That list of biblical characters found in Hebrews 11? They weren't perfect.

Noah got drunk.
Abraham lied about his wife to save his own skin.
Jacob could be a real jerk.
Rahab was a prostitute.
Moses killed a man.

But God used them anyway.

And God can use *us* in any way. He wants to, and we need him to for our lives to mean something. Can you think of places in your life where God's grace and faithfulness have flowed through you to bring him the glory?

God's grace and faithfulness have flowed through my parents their whole lives. My dad is a retired ophthalmologist, and my mom was his surgical nurse. We never went on vacations growing up because every year Mom and Dad would go on a mission trip and take a kid or two along. I was able to go with them to Zimbabwe, and we served at a Baptist hospital named Sanyati in the African bush. It was so far out, they didn't have many eye doctors come and visit, so Mom and Dad were doing surgery almost daily. One day, a missionary from one of the larger cities came for a visit and told us that word had gotten around that Jesus had come to Sanyati. Jesus, as the gossip chain went, was a bald-headed American with a big smile who was as kind as the Bible described. And he was here, helping the blind to see!

Needless to say, the missionary took one look at my dad and doubled over in laughter. Hysterical, tears-out-of-his-eyes laughter. He thought it was great. Dad fit the physical description perfectly, and with some relief, immediately put two and two together. Dad, on the other hand, was *mortified*. He had been praying with each patient and telling them about the love of Jesus, and somewhere along the way, the message had gotten lost in translation the farther it traveled into the villages. The point is this: Dad was bringing glory to God through faithfully serving him. We quickly cleared up any misconceptions and made sure everyone knew that Jesus *had not* in fact returned, but that it was just some bald guy from America with a big smile who loved Jesus and was trying his best to introduce others to the real Son of God.

God still uses his people, and he wants to use you too. Why? Because faith brings obedience, and obedience helps us live the way we were meant to live. Stop for a second and apply this to your life. How can you be obedient to the Lord this week? Is he calling you to do something? How can he use you for his glory?

When you are steadfast and unwavering in how God wants you to live, he *will* use you. He created you to have a relationship with him and to point others to him. That's why you're here. When you live out your faith in Christ, you are living out your destiny. So, put on your armor of God, and pick up that shield of faith. That kind of clothing is way cooler than wearing any jacket.

Chapter Question

What are ways you can "up your game" as you live out your faith with the people around you?

Chapter Twenty-One

WISDOM VS. FOOLISHNESS

The other day I opened up the pantry because I wanted some crunch with my coffee, and there it was—a glorious lone granola bar in a clear zipped baggie. I'd eaten half the package a few days before and saved the rest rather than throwing it away. I was proud of myself for thinking ahead and putting it in such an obvious place where I would see it. So, I opened it up, and with a little more glee than it was worthy of, I took a bite.

You guys, it was *horrible.*

Not because it wasn't an amazing peanut butter granola bar awaiting my enjoyment. It was horrible because in my extreme thoughtfulness of saving it, I'd placed my amazing peanut butter granola bar directly on top of a bowl of *fresh garlic bulbs.*

My amazing peanut butter granola bar had been infused with the pungent and earthy flavor of something that belongs in spaghetti. Let me assure you, these are *not* complementary flavors. Solomon drops a lot of wisdom in Ecclesiastes, and it holds a verse that talks about what happened to my granola bar *and* what happens to us when we are careless of where we place our minds, hearts, and souls. Ecclesiastes 10:1 says, "As dead flies give perfume a bad smell, so a little folly outweighs wisdom and honor."

I can look back and see my own foolishness when I placed my amazing peanut butter life choices upon some nasty, pungent garlic cloves of stupidity. I wasn't evil, but I certainly wasn't wise. Instead of living my life intentionally, I just let life live me. That never goes well, by the way.

Dr. Henry Cloud says there are three types of people in the world: Wise, Foolish, and Evil.[66] (You can google this idea; there is a lot of stuff out there on it. I highly recommend checking it out; it makes a lot of sense!) I am not evil, but I have been foolish many times and never want to live that way again. Actually, I pray for godly wisdom all the time. I'm thinking you may be in this boat on some level too, so in this chapter I want to define foolishness and wisdom. Once godly wisdom is examined, we will have a more defined vision of how to live lives of faithfulness, obedience, and wise intentionality.

Deuteronomy 32 occurs at the end of Moses's life. Joshua is about to take over and lead the people into the promised land. It is Moses's swan song—literally a song he recited to the people of Israel before his death. In the song it mentions all the ways the Lord was a God of providence and deliverance to his people and contrasts it to the Israelites' belligerence and unfaithfulness to God while in the desert. In Deuteronomy 32:6 Moses asks the people, "Is this the way you repay the Lord, you foolish and unwise people?"

That word for foolish in Hebrew is *nabal*. Does that sound familiar? It should if you are familiar with David's wife, Abigail. Before David, she was married to a self-absorbed man who lived out his name. (First Samuel 25 tells you the whole story, but verse 25 tells us Nabal means "fool.") The original Hebraic word has a physical picture and means to wear out, crumble, wither, fall, or fade. When Moses called the people foolish, it was in direct contrast to God's covenant under which they had been living. A few moments earlier, in Deuteronomy 29:2–6, Moses said the following:

Your eyes have seen all that the Lord did in Egypt to Pharaoh, to all his officials and to all his land. With your own eyes you saw those great trials, those signs and great wonders. But to this day the Lord has not given you a mind that understands or eyes that see or ears that hear. Yet the Lord says, "During the forty years that I led you through the wilderness, your clothes did not wear out, nor did the sandals on your feet. You ate no bread and drank no wine or other fermented drink. I did this so that you might know that I am the Lord your God."

In the Bible, foolishness runs the gamut from sheer stupidity to wickedness. Either way, foolishness is destructive, and it will *wear you out*. In New Testament Greek, the word for foolish means a thoughtlessness or lack of intelligence. When describing the "foolish" virgins in the parable of the bridesmaids (Matthew 25), the Greek adjective used is the basis for our word *moron*.[67]

Wisdom, however, is the antithesis of that concept, and in Greek means "learned, cultivated, skilled, or clever." In Hebrew, wisdom means "someone who can judge correctly and follow the best course of action." It is a combination of knowing and doing.

I want us to compare foolishness with wisdom and get an easy visual picture of what the Bible says about both. Here are just a few verses on the subject:

The wise in heart accept commands, but a chattering fool comes to ruin (Proverbs 10:8–9).

A fool finds pleasure in wicked schemes, but a person of understanding delights in wisdom (Proverbs 10:23).

Fools give full vent to their rage, but the wise bring calm in the end (Proverbs 29:11).

These verses describe ways we can react that are wise and ways we can react that are foolish. Are there any reactions that tempt you in the foolish category? If so, start praying for God to embody the wise counterpart and reaction in your life. Any foolish attributes you struggle with don't have to define you anymore. Just because we have been foolish in the past does not mean that is who we are. We can stop today and strive to live in godly wisdom through the power of the Holy Spirit. It's not about perfection; it's about obedience!

James 3:13–16 says:

Who is wise and understanding among you? Let them show it by their good life, by deeds done in the humility that comes from wisdom. But if you harbor bitter envy and selfish ambition in your hearts, do not boast about it or deny the truth. Such "wisdom" does not come down from heaven but is earthly, unspiritual, demonic. For where you have envy and selfish ambition, there you find disorder and every evil practice.

The verses give us a few ways to live out wisdom. They also point out that earthly wisdom is far inferior to God's wisdom. It even calls earthly wisdom unspiritual and demonic.

Let *that* one sink in a minute!

James 3:17–18 continues on and lists out some benefits of Godly wisdom:

> But the wisdom that comes from heaven is first of all pure; then peace-loving, considerate, submissive, full of mercy and good fruit, impartial and sincere. Peacemakers who sow in peace reap a harvest of righteousness.

Did you notice that the positive aspects of wisdom don't just stay with wisdom? They permeate into your own personality, defining your outlook, defining your virtues through the power of the Holy Spirit.

A wise life brings so many benefits. In fact, the entire second chapter of Proverbs recites the benefits of wisdom. Proverbs 2:1–5 tell us if we...

> Accept God's Word,
>> Store up his commands,
>>> Turn our ears to wisdom,
>>>> Apply our heart to understanding,
>>>>> Call out for insight,
>>>>>> Cry aloud for understanding,
>>>>>>> Look for wisdom like treasure...

"...then you will understand the fear of the Lord and find the knowledge of God."

Don't miss that the above is an if/then statement. For an outcome to happen, something previous has to occur. We know that when we ask the Lord for wisdom, we will understand what is "right and just and fair" (Proverbs 2:9). But it even goes further than that. Check out these benefits of finding wisdom.

> Wisdom will enter our hearts.
> > Knowledge will be pleasant to our soul.
> > > Discretion will protect us.
> > > > Understanding will guard us.
> > > > > Wisdom will save us from the ways of the wicked.

When we strive to live a life of wisdom, we are humble children scampering with excitement into the lap of God, who created the universe and everything in it. He is our protector and provider. When we seek wisdom, we are choosing to learn from the Ultimate Wisdom who is full of grace and truth. It is good for us to always remember Isaiah 55:9–8: "'For my thoughts are not your thoughts, neither are your ways my ways,' declares the Lord. 'As the heavens are higher than the earth, so are my ways higher than your ways and my thoughts than your thoughts.'"

A wisdom-filled life is living in God's ways and not our own. We are trusting in his Word, his will, and his ways to guide us into the life we were created to live. Choosing wisdom is choosing to live out our destiny as believers. End today by asking the Lord for wisdom in every area of your life. He gives good gifts to his people.

Chapter Questions

How have you found the Hebrew definition of foolishness to be true in your life?

How are wisdom and wise choices the stronger path?

Chapter Twenty-Two

THE WISDOM IN FEAR

Fear can be a common bondage for us all. We fear for our children, our marriages, our health, our safety, our relationships. We fear if what we said came out wrong, if what we did was misinterpreted, and we fear if our perceptions are, in fact, reality. We fear if we are too late, too soon, or too much. Anxiety looms and instead of covering ourselves with God's love and grace, we find ourselves covered and cowering in fear. Fear of the unknown. Fear of the future. Fear of missing out. Fear of people. It's what I call "negative fear," and part of the reason we experience it is because we think we are in control. And that is exactly where Satan and his minions wants us.

But there is another kind of fear, and it is the wiser lens of which we should view our lives. It helps focus our minds, define our hearts, and gives clarity to the way we choose to treat others. When we live in what I call "positive fear"…

We
Can't
Be
Stopped.

Positive fear is fear of the Lord. When our minds are set on fearing the Lord, God's kingdom brings freedom to our souls, and the evil of insecurity does not sway our decisions. Wisdom reigns, and relational hierarchy between the created and the creator is in the right order.

When we experience negative fear, wisdom goes out the window. Do you know that where we operate from in our brains actually shifts when we are afraid? We move from logical thinking to the fight or flight mentality. Negative fear can make us act foolishly, emotionally, and irrationally. It pulls us away from our Creator and makes us feel alone. When we live in "positive fear"—the way we were *created* to live—wisdom rushes in like a wave in the ocean. The more we live in fear of the Lord, the more the tide continues to bless us with a consistent rhythm of refreshment.

Check out just a handful of the benefits the Bible mentions we receive when we fear the Lord:

The fear of the Lord is the beginning of knowledge (Proverbs 1:7).
The fear of the Lord adds length to life (Proverbs 10:27).
Those who fear the Lord have a secure fortress (Proverbs 14:26).
The fear of the Lord is a fountain of life (Proverbs 14:27).
Salvation is near those who fear the Lord (Psalm 85:9).
God's mercy is extended to those who fear him (Luke 1:50).

We can even see a corporate example of "positive fear" in Acts 9:31. It's after the conversion of Saul to Paul, "the church throughout Judea, Galilee and Samaria enjoyed a time of peace and was strengthened. Living in the fear of the Lord and encouraged by the Holy Spirit, it increased in numbers."[68]

The word used for fear in the above verse is *phobos* in Greek. It means to fear, withdraw, flee, or avoid.[69] That's great, but that obviously isn't what this verse is talking about. If the church had withdrawn from or avoided the Lord, it never would have made it a week, much less a few millennia. That would have been negative fear.

The fear this verse references is obviously what we are calling positive fear because it is linked to being encouraged from the Holy Spirit. When we look at this verse in its cultural context, the dissonance is removed. The believers referred to here (those who lived in Judea, Galilee, and even those considered "half-Hebrew" in Samaria) are of Jewish origin. The word fear in Hebrew is *Yirat*, and it is all over the Old Testament when referring to God.

Remember, the biblical Hebrew language is limited to just 8000 words, and one word meant several different things. Yirat is a great example of that concept. Yirat can mean *to be afraid* or *to draw away from*, which would be reacting in negative fear. But… it also can mean *to revere* or *be drawn toward* in awe, which is positive fear when related to the Lord. So, to be clear, using the definitions above:

- Negative fear = to be afraid, to draw away from
- Positive fear = to revere, to be drawn toward in awe

I deeply desire for you to live in fear. That's a weird statement, isn't it? I want you to freely abide in fearing the Lord because there is wisdom in it. Proverbs 2 reveals wisdom and fear of the Lord are joined together. You want to be wise? Fear the Lord. Do you fear the Lord? You will grow in wisdom.

There is a great if/then statement in the first five verses of Proverbs 2. It says something like this:

IF…

You accept my words,

    Store up my commands within you,

        Listen to wisdom,

            Apply your heart to understanding,

                Call out for insight,

                    Search for wisdom like treasure...

THEN... You will understand what it means to fear the Lord.

Fearing the Lord absolutely has an element of being terrified, but even that is positive because we are up close and personal with our Creator. It also keeps us on track and makes us think twice before choosing to sin. Society has made God so casual that we have lost the awareness of his glory, holiness, and awesome power. The prophets Daniel (Daniel 8:17), Ezekiel (Ezekiel 1:26–28), and the disciple John (Revelation 1:9–18) all found themselves face down and trembling because they were overwhelmed by the presence of the Lord. They also were acutely aware of their sin compared to God's perfection. God is holy—above and beyond us, choosing to reach down and interact with us—and that can be overwhelming. To see God in his glory puts humanity in our place. We realize he is God, and we are not. It is the hierarchy of creation. We are at his mercy, totally reliant on him.

So many times, we get caught up in what we can see, and we gloss over the deeper and unseen spiritual realm. We allow the *created* to trump the *eternal* because it can be seen and touched. Our priorities get out of whack, which leads to our lives getting out of whack.

Instead of fearing our Creator, we fear the created.

The creation hierarchy is flipped on its head when we fear the created over the Creator. After all, the definition of idolatry is putting something over God. When we fear the social ramifications of others, or what they will say or do, over what God says or does, not only is it easier to fall into sin but without knowing it, we are *creating an idol.*

The Hebrew language has several words that can mean idol, but I'd like to point out three—*atsabh*, *etseb*, and *otseb*. They all mean "a cause of grief"![70] When we struggle with fear of what the created can do to us, it does indeed cause serious grief. Sometimes stepping back and realizing that I am acting like something has power over the God of the Universe is enough to snap me out of it. Nothing is bigger, or stronger, or more awesome than our God.

Fearing God isn't about being terrified. Psalm 34:4 states, "I sought the Lord, and he answered me; he delivered me from all my fears." Fearing the Lord is about revering and worshipping in awe. Did you notice no one who sees God in the Bible runs away? They may hit the floor face first, pass out, or ramble on with nervous energy, but they all *stay*. They worship. They know what to do because the desire to worship the Lord is inside all of us. We were created to bow and praise the Living God. When we worship, the initial terror goes away, and we are left with comfort, peace, confident assurance, and joy. True worship forms a deep connection with the God of the Universe.

Living in awe of the Lord is loving him by how we live. Solomon in all his wisdom finishes the book of Ecclesiastes (NLT) with this little gem: "Here now is my final conclusion: Fear God and obey his commands, for this is everyone's duty."

That pretty much puts it in a nutshell, doesn't it?

By obeying the commands of God, we take part in both aspects of fearing the Lord—remembering that he is a powerful, mighty, awesome being who is above and beyond us. We remember who is in ultimate control as our Creator (fearing) and worshipping and pulling close to him because of it (revering). Living in fear of the Lord is two sides of the same coin, and it is important to define and understand how they work together to create a balanced view of our amazing and infinite God.

If you'd really like to put this idea into practice, jot down a few ways you can live in fear of the Lord today. Be intentional about it.

Then, ask the Lord to give you the strength and awareness of his presence to live it out.

Chapter Question

How would you compare positive fear and negative fear?

Chapter Twenty-Three

WISDOM IN HUMILITY

Humility is vastly underrated, but I don't think it cares. In our world of sarcasm, overconfidence, and brazen manipulation, a humble attitude seems like an obscure and foreign concept. Somehow everyone has believed the lie that humility is weakness. Sassy has become equated with cool, and insults are awarded with laughter. How many times have you experienced someone being mean or prideful, possibly followed by smug grins, or even seen high fives all round?

Because society isn't clear on the definition of humility, people will self-efface in an attempt to be humble. Low self-esteem is not humility. Neither is beating yourself up to bring down something the Lord has done through you. The Bible sees things in a different light, and we need to be enlightened so we can experience this joy only found in and through Christ.

To continue the idea that fearing the Lord should be a priority, Proverbs 15:33 (NLT) meshes reverence and humility. It says: "Fear of the Lord teaches wisdom; humility precedes honor." Don't you just love it when Scripture puts concepts together?

According to this verse, wisdom lived out brings honor. Did you catch what comes after living a life of wisdom, but *before* honor?

Humility.

For our minds to continue to process this, it must be noted that wisdom brings humility, but the reverse is also true. Check out Proverbs 11:2. It says, "When pride comes, then comes disgrace, but with humility comes wisdom."

To get a good visual of this, I want you to draw a straight arrow between wisdom and humility below, with the arrow pointing toward humility. Directly under that, reverse it, and draw an arrow pointing toward wisdom. See how you just made an equal sign? Wisdom and humility are equated because in the Bible, one is not found without the other.

WISDOM   HUMILITY

Solomon was wise until he started worshipping other gods, and then he was led astray (1 Kings 11:4). Moses is described as the most humble man on earth (Numbers 12:3), but he wasn't allowed to enter the promised land because he struck a rock for water rather than speaking to it as the Lord had required. Adam and Eve ate from the tree of knowledge to get wisdom rather than humbly obeying their Creator God (Genesis 3:6). Like it or not, wisdom and humility are not mutually exclusive.

What is the biblical sense of humility? It is defined as "a personal quality where someone shows dependence on God and respect for others."[71] Does this definition sound familiar to you? Maybe something you've heard in church? Jesus reiterates it when he answers the question of "What is the greatest commandment?" in Matthew 22:37–39.

According to Jesus, the greatest commandment is to love God and love others.

In biblical times, the first part—to love God—was a well-known concept. Jesus was referring to part of the Shema, which is Deuteronomy 6:4–7. It says we are to love the Lord with all our heart, soul, and strength. But the second part of his answer surprised his listeners. It was taken from a somewhat obscure verse in Leviticus 19:18. Sadly, the whole idea of loving others came out of left field for many of the temple leaders.

Living in humility is living in wisdom, and that wisdom is gleaned from the word of God. We must know and live out the fact that God is God; we are not. We are to love and serve him all the days of our lives. Yet again in James 3:13 you see wisdom and humility partnering together. It says, "Who is wise and understanding among you? Let them show it by their good life, by deeds done in the humility that comes from wisdom."

It is important to note the Greek word translated as "to show" in James 3:13 is *deiknumi*, and it can also be translated "to demonstrate, exhibit, or make known."[72] By living a God-honoring life and doing good works out of a humble spirit, we exhibit wisdom that comes from the Lord. Wisdom is partnered with humility.

We have a friend who has done rather well in business. His heart is for the Lord, and he strives to obediently serve him each day. He is constantly giving above and beyond his tithe, and he helps kids go to camp who couldn't afford to otherwise. He assists missionaries who are stateside who need housing while in America and does so much more for so many people. He wants no accolades or attention or for even people to know who he is. He is completely humble, knowing that he is sharing his blessings from the Lord with others. He embodies the idea of wisdom and humility from the James verse we read earlier.

This theme of wisdom and humility is echoed again in Micah 6:8, which we talked about a few chapters ago. To bring it back to our minds, here it is again:

He has shown you, O mortal, what is good. And what does the Lord require of you? To act justly and to love mercy and to walk humbly with your God.

There is so much in this verse. Before, we focused on the word *require*. This time, I want us to break it down further. My hope is that you will personalize certain things and feel them in your soul. To start, mark out the words "O mortal" and write your name above it.

That's already more personal, isn't it?

The Hebrew word for "good" used here is *towb*, and it means something that is pleasant or agreeable.[73] It also can mean something that functions properly.[74] Do you want your life to be pleasant? Do you want it to function the way God intended? Then read Micah 6:8 again and see how the Lord tells us we should live.

Now we get to the word *require* again.
Yes, it is *still there*.

The things listed after the word require are not optional for a Christ-follower. We are about to be told what God is looking for in a true believer. This is big. Feel it, pray for it in your life, and seek these things with all your heart. To grow in wisdom and faith and goodness, we are required to:

- Act justly.
- Love mercy.
- Walk humbly with God.

The first two things the Lord requires of us deal with how we interact with our fellow man, and even then, a sense of biblical humility exists in both attributes. The last requirement deals with how we interact with the Lord. He requires us to walk humbly with him as believers.

When we depend on the Lord, self-centered ego no longer leads our life. The will of the Lord is first and foremost on our minds and in our hearts. Depending on God means we know he is judge, not us. He is in control, not us. His will is perfect, not ours. Everything we have in our being yields to him. And instead of this binding us up, it brings freedom. We no longer are bound by worry, fear, or concern about controlling situations.

Philippians 2:1–4 explains how we should live in humility the same way Jesus did. It says, (emphasis mine):

Therefore if you have any *encouragement* from being united with Christ, if any *comfort* from his love, if any *common sharing in the Spirit*, if any *tenderness and compassion*, then make my joy complete by being like-minded, having the same love, being one in spirit and of one mind. Do nothing out of selfish ambition or vain conceit. Rather, in humility value others above yourselves, not looking to your own interests but each of you to the interests of the others.

To apply this to our lives, take the words that are blessings we receive from Jesus and turn them into how we can bless others through a spirit of humility. Really personalize your answers to your life situations. What are your gifts? Talents? God-given abilities that will make you a funnel of Christ's love to others? Ask yourself,

- How can I encourage others?
- How can I comfort others?

- How can I find fellowship in the spirit?
- How can I show tenderness and compassion?

Philippians 2:5–18 continues to walk us through a lesson in how to depend on God and show respect to others. One of my repeated themes when I speak is this:

> Your life isn't *about* you. It's about God *in* you.

When we realize that truth and live it out, the freedom that humility brings flows into our hearts. We need to stop *trying* to be humble and, instead, start *living* in humility. You are here for a reason and a purpose, and God gifted you uniquely so your life can bring him glory. Don't you desire that? I know I do. In the end, humility is making God your everything and knowing that he has you in his hands. It is trusting that he is God, and you are not. It is living in the right kind of fear of the Lord. It is living in wisdom. It is living in confidence and joy. Humility is strong and loving and secure.

Who knew humility was so awesome, right?

Chapter Question

Why are wisdom and humility not mutually exclusive?

Chapter Twenty-Four

WISDOM AND JOY

C ory and I recently built a swing bed using Pinterest plans and raw planks of wood. A swing bed, if you're not familiar, is like a hammock on steroids. We hung ours in our sunroom—so we can see all those turkeys I told you about—and it is perfect. It's fluffy, snuggly, swing-y, and crazy comfortable. The downside is once we're there, I never want to leave. I find myself completely content, tucked under a blanket, swinging with a cup of tea and a book, and could stay that way for a few decades. Granted, because we built it together, there are emotional ties but combine that with the physical comfort it offers and, well… I want to remain there for a long, long time.

Remain.

John 15:7–11 uses the word *remain* five times in these verses. The word remain comes from the root verb *meno*, which can be defined as to remain, abide, or stay.[75] And to really get this concept into our brain, *Merriam-Webster* defines the word *remain* as "to continue unchanged."[76] To remain is not temporary.

Remain is *not* a show-up-and-leave kind of word.

It is to be present. When we see a word repeated that close together in Scripture, we need to understand what is being emphasized. John 15 is talking about bearing spiritual fruit in the life of a believer. For us to be fruitful—useful and fulfilling our purpose in the kingdom of God—we must remain in Jesus. These verses build and point out something we can easily miss. In verse 11, Jesus himself gives two reasons why we should remain, remain, remain in him.

1. We remain so his joy can be in us.
2. We remain so our joy may be complete.

God is our only source of true joy, which is a fruit of the spirit. When we remain in him, we will bear fruit. Verse 11 actually refers back to verse 10, which has the feel of an if/then statement. It says, "If you keep my commands, (then) you will remain in my love…"

Did you catch that? By remaining in a relationship and keeping the commands we have been given, our joy will be complete. It's like "remaining" fertilizes our fruit.

I love the comparison that is assumed. God has so much joy that he can give it infinitely to each of us when we stay connected to his Spirit. Even when he shares it, he has more than we could ever handle. Our joy is complete, yet he has storehouses left to spare!

Do you know someone who overflows with joy? Immediately, my mom comes to mind. When I was growing up, she always had a smile on her face. She's kind of known for it in my hometown. My mom reads her bible every day, and I have so many memories of coming home from school and seeing her with her bible on her lap. When I was in seminary, which was before Google, *she* was my Google. That woman knew more Scripture by memory than anyone else I've ever known. I could call her and ask for verses on anything, and she could quote at least five on the spot.

My mom now suffers from dementia, and I'm not sure she could quote even one verse anymore. But it is in her heart, and it still shines through her attitude. Even with the dimming of her mind, she still shines with the joy of the Lord. I know not all dementia patients have that, but I am so thankful my mom does.

The Greek word for joy is *chara*, and it describes inner gladness and delight. It is happiness or gladness caused by a spiritual reality rather than the cause of human circumstance. Joy is deep-soul pleasure that manifests itself in a person's attitude and behavior.[77]

This definition makes complete sense when paired with John 15. When we choose to live our lives under the authority and protection of the Lord, of course we are going to experience the joy of being with him. How could we not? Our temporary worries pass away and we have an inner confidence that God is on his throne and in control.

What a relief and joy it is to know that our life doesn't depend on us, but instead on the spirit of God living in and through us. That really takes the pressure off, doesn't it! Like Jesus said, his joy will be in us and our joy will be complete. Galatians 5:22–23 supports this thought, "The fruit of the spirit is love, JOY, peace, forbearance, kindness, goodness, faithfulness, gentleness, and self-control…"

Joy does involve an element of happiness because there is contentment. It comes from us remaining on the vine, which brings us close to the Lord and the knowledge that he meets our every need. Remember, fruit of the spirit is different than spiritual gifts. Different people have different gifts to build up the kingdom of God. But Christians have the ability through the spirit of God in their lives to experience all the fruit— the evidence—of God's spirit inside of them.

When we remain close to our Savior and live in his ways, God blesses us. Again, we see the theme of wisdom, but this time it is paired with joy. Ecclesiastes 2:25–26 (NLT) tells us God gives wisdom, knowledge, and joy to the person who pleases him.

Wisdom and joy are a natural pairing, just like being foolish and miserable go hand in hand. When we live in wisdom, we remain in God's will. It's no secret that God's will is not always easy—many times it is much more difficult than sin—but God's will always bring joy with it. Why? *Because we are living the way the Lord intended us to live.*

Psalm 16:11 shows us that when we live in wisdom and stay close to the Lord and his ways, we will find joy. It's one of my all-time favorite bible verses, and it says,

You make known to me the path of life; you will fill me with joy in your presence, with eternal pleasures at your right hand.

All three of the things above denote movement toward and close proximity to the Father. The path of life is being wise and walking in his ways. We have joy in his presence because we are remaining in him. And, when we remain, we find joy close by at his right hand. Being close to the Father means we will choose to live in his will for our lives. There is no room for unforgiveness, resentment, or bitterness when your heart is full. None of those things can coexist with joy.

We need to realize that another Greek word is closely related to Chara (joy) by its root. The word is *Charis*. Sound familiar? It is the Greek word for grace.

We find joy by living in the grace given to us through Jesus Christ. Listen friend, when you placed your sin at the foot of the cross, you were forgiven. You are cherished and free and the Holy Spirit is inside you. Now, through his presence and power, you are to extend that grace to others. Extending grace is a part of who God is, and it should be a part of who you are. When you extend grace to others, you will receive joy from the Lord. But take note...

If you refuse to live in grace, you will never live in joy.

The power of the Holy Spirit gives us the ability to offer grace, even if it is outside our power to do so. Joy comes to us not when things are great but when we remain in our great God. By abiding in him, our lives become fruitful for his kingdom. We have complete hope and faith that God is in control, and we understand that we must offer the same grace that has been given to us through Christ. So, hunt for joy. Seek it like treasure. Give grace freely, because joy comes back to you in the process. Above all, remain with the Father and live out his will for your life. Snuggle in, friend, because that is where true joy is found.

Chapter Question

Why must a person live in grace to find joy?

Chapter Twenty-Five

PEACE

A few days ago, Cory and I went with shopping with our daughter, Elizabeth, who needed some new jeans. Once in the store, Cory headed to the men's section, and Elizabeth and I wandered over to the women's side. After about five minutes, I see my husband yelling something across the store and waving his arms like he's in a swarm of bees. His eyes were as big as saucers. Once we got within earshot, I heard the words none of us ever want to hear: "There's been a shooting! We've got to go to the back of the store!"

We walked quickly into the storeroom and waited while a few others entered after us. A mom and her child got behind us and squatted down using a steel clothing dolly as a shield. Once all ten customers were inside the room, they locked the door and escorted us to the lounge area where the employees take breaks. We stayed there for an hour and a half until we were escorted to our car by eight lovely linebacker-sized gentlemen with huge guns—both literal and metaphorical—who were sporting camo, Kevlar vests, and full tactical gear.

A shoe company was debuting a new style of sneaker that day, and some guys began fighting over them in line in the mall. Things escalated, and they started shooting at each other. One person was injured; many were traumatized. We didn't hear the shots but were still somewhat shaken.

The day shattered before us. We felt disheveled, and our bodies were stuck in a whirlwind of emotions. The shooters were still on the loose. Have you ever been so stressed and fragmented that you can't make sense of your thoughts? Even after calming down and realizing we were safe, it was a crazy feeling. And I bet you can guess what we prayed for…

Peace.

Just the word has a calming effect, doesn't it? The Hebrew definition of peace meets every desire when we feel segmented, scattered, conflicted, and just plain old not put together. It's what we desired in the mall that day and something I know you have prayed for in your life as well. The Hebrew word for peace has two meanings that go hand in hand, but the overarching theme of how to have peace can be seen clearly in Isaiah 26:3 when it says, "You will keep in perfect peace those whose minds are steadfast, because they trust in you."

To break this down a bit, this verse says that those whose minds are steadfast, which is a definition of faithful, will be kept in perfect peace. The faithful will be kept in perfect peace because they trust in the Lord.

The Hebrew word used for trust here is *batach*. It conveys a picture of clinging to something or someone. It also can be translated for the word *secure* or *security*.[78] This verse tells us that when we cling to the Lord and are faithful in our relationship with him, we will find peace in the Lord no matter the circumstance.

Can you think of a time when you experienced God's peace, possibly in a crazy circumstance?

As you may know, the Hebrew word for peace is *shalom*. Today in Israel, shalom is used as a greeting, a goodbye, and general well-wishes to anyone you may see during the day. In Israel, you hear it all the time. The meaning behind shalom is full of kindness, and it wishes someone a state of wholeness, for wholeness is one definition of shalom. Completeness is another. This verse is saying those who are steadfast in trusting the Lord will be kept in complete wholeness. No matter what our mistakes or past sins may be, our fragmented life can be repaired and made new in Christ when we trust in him.

The meaning of peace doesn't stop there. To add a deeper dimension to shalom, another meaning of shalom is "restoration; making right through a payment or restitution."[79] This is what Paul meant in Ephesians 2:14 when he refers to Jesus as our peace.

The sacrificial death and resurrection of Jesus can restore our souls, making broken humans whole when we believe in him. Our peace begins with the belief that Jesus paid for our sins on the cross. The prophetic words of Isaiah 53:5 again shows this to be true, "The punishment that brought us *peace* was on him, and by his wounds we are healed." To make that stick, we could rephrase that with the other definition of peace and say, "The punishment that brought us *restoration* was on him, and by his wounds we are healed."

Wow, right?

Jesus, the Lamb of God who sacrificed himself for us, is our peace. He is our restitution that made our broken relationship with our Father complete. Sin separated; Jesus restored. Nothing else can make us whole. Jesus stressed this very point to his disciples hours before he died when he said, "Peace I leave with you; my peace I give you. I do not give to you as the world gives. Do not let your hearts be troubled and do not be afraid" (John 14:27).

Jesus left them with peace. And, boy, did they need it in all the crucifixion chaos. Jesus went even further when he pointed out the peace he was leaving wasn't like what the world had to offer. His peace was bigger. Better. Not what they were expecting but so much deeper. He knew they were going to be troubled, so he didn't leave them empty-handed.

The Greek word used here for troubled is *tarasso*, and it means to agitate back and forth, to shake to and fro, or to set in motion that which is supposed to be still.[80] As women, we know that feeling all too well. Our hearts get shaken, agitated, and all in a whirl when we were created to be still in rest, peace, and assurance that the Lord is in control. As a wife, mom, daughter, and friend, I can think of all kinds of things that threaten my peace. But just as he did for his disciples, Jesus provides peace for us too. If you have asked Jesus into your heart, the Spirit that brings peace lives inside you. It is powerful and mighty and brings wholeness and restoration. Our job is to stop attempting to be in control and to look to the Creator, who is in ultimate control.

Philippians 4:6–7 says, "Do not be anxious about anything, but in every situation, by prayer and petition, with thanksgiving, present your requests to God. And the peace of God, which transcends all understanding, will guard your hearts and your minds in Christ Jesus."

Did you catch the three ways we are to bring our requests to God?

1. By prayer
2. By petition
3. With thanksgiving

Petition, or supplication, is praying for a specific, deeply felt need. You know the prayers that come from that deep ache in your being? That's this kind of prayer. The Greek word is *deesis* and describes a heartfelt prayer that comes out of a place of lacking.[81] And the thanksgiving comes into play because we know that God is not lacking in any area. He's got it covered, and we are in his hands.

Verse 7 above says God gives peace that transcends anything we can understand. That word *transcend* means to rise above or be superior to.[82] We can't comprehend peace, but we have been given the gift of experiencing it. God hears our prayers, petitions, and thankfulness, and in his holiness makes us complete in Christ over and over again.

To find peace in relationships, we first must be at peace with ourselves. Once we have peace, we are able to widen the circle and bring it into our relationships. God is the author of peace, not other people.

But, man, can other people steal our peace if we let them! Do you know we have a way to combat that very issue? Proverbs 16:7 assures us, "When the Lord takes pleasure in anyone's way, he causes their enemies to make peace with them."

So, live in faithfulness. Cling to the Lord. Allow him to restore your life. He offers his peace to us every day, no matter the circumstance.

Chapter Questions

How is the definition of peace as "complete wholeness" different than the more secular understanding of simply "a lack of conflict"?

How are they similar, and how do they differ?

Chapter Twenty-Six

BE STILL

How do you act when you feel angry, stressed, or anxious? When I am really bothered, I clean.

I don't mean I clean like a normal person. It's more like a Tasmanian devil. My kitchen will sparkle. Laundry gets done. Floors get swept, shelves get dusted, everything gets put in its place. If I hit the baseboards, watch out. I'm about an inch from losing my ever-loving mind! I don't know if it is busyness fed by nervous energy or if I'm attempting to control my environment to get a handle on things. Whatever it is, it makes me feel a little bit better. But if someone tries to stop me in the middle of my mild-yet-below-the-surface freak-out, I immediately balk at the idea. Stop? Why would I stop? I am doing great with whatever is bothering me, thank you.

When someone in the Bible says, "Be still," it's never easy for the hearer to do. We know it's important because that phrase is seen in Scripture several distinct times. Each time, God's people were feeling… bothered. And each time, a different Hebrew or Greek word is used. In the Bible, when "be still" is said, it always seems illogical. But it is also when God's people needed to experience stillness the most.

You may be much calmer than I when you get upset, but if you ever find yourself in somewhat of a tizzy, let me encourage you to think of the first seven verses found in Psalm 37. I've underlined some phrases that the author David tells us to do:

Do not fret because of those who are evil or be envious of those who do wrong; for like the grass they will soon wither, like green plants they will soon die away. Trust in the Lord and do good; dwell in the land and enjoy safe pasture. Take delight in the Lord, and he will give you the desires of your heart. Commit your way to the Lord; trust in him and he will do this: He will make your righteous reward shine like the dawn, your vindication like the noonday sun. Be still before the Lord and wait patiently for him; do not fret when people succeed in their ways, when they carry out their wicked schemes.

In Hebrew, that last sentence doesn't start with "be still" like it does in English. Instead, it uses a variation of the Hebrew word *damam* that can be translated as "rest." The long definition of damam adds "to be or grow silent or still,"[83] giving us our English translation of be still.

If you've ever seen kids playing the game red light/green light, you know people can be still—as in not moving—but not be *at rest*. They can be tense as a polecat and twice as excited while never moving a muscle. Thus, we can already see this advice of "be still" is not a tense moment frozen in anxiety. It is referring to a restful, confident stillness, one that finds rest in the Lord.

When we are tense, it can be hard to rest in the Lord. We want to fret, fix, or fixate on whatever is bothering us. These verses, however, give us advice on a better way to handle our anxiety. Don't fret. Trust and delight in the Lord. Commit your way to him. Rest your mind.

After David tells us to "rest" he chases it with a "and wait patiently." He puts rest and patience together. When you think about it, we really can't have one without the other, can we? This idea of waiting patiently comes from a form of the Hebrew verb *chuwl*. It means to whirl, dance, or writhe.[84] Weird, right? Now would be a great time for us to examine the context of this definition.

If we plug in one explanation of the word chuwl and read this as "Be still and writhe as in pain or fear," it doesn't really make sense. Why would David, the author, tell us to rest but then tell us to wait painfully in the same breath? Remember when I told you there's not a lot of Hebrew words in the Bible, so one word means multiple things? This is a great example of that. The reader must look at context to figure it out. Let's look at a different part of the definition.

To whirl or dance is a lot different than writhing in pain... unless someone is a *really* bad dancer! If we read that same sentence using the definition of dancing in mind, the mental picture is for us to rest and yet dance before the Lord without a worry or care in the world. Can you feel the freedom and lack of worry in the situation? That is the idea here!

Dancing was a form of worship we see in the Old Testament. David danced before the Lord when he was bringing the ark into Jerusalem (2 Samuel 6:14). Miriam danced in worship after Pharaoh was drowned in the sea (Exodus 15:20–21), and in the Psalms (Psalm 30 to be exact), wailing is turned into dancing because of what the Lord has done. Dancing shows freedom. Dancing shows joy.

We are not only to rest in the Lord but celebrate what he is going to do in our lives. While we rest and wait, he wants our hearts to be free to move and swell with grace and confidence without worry or fear. This concept continues to build even more because this verse also tells us not to fret.

The Hebrew word for fret is *charas*, not to be confused with the Greek word *charis*, meaning grace. In fact, their definitions couldn't be further apart! Hebrew *charah* means to burn with anger, or one who is hot.[85] This verse alone tells us to rest, don't worry, and don't fret.

It makes me think of the viral video of the little boy who was about five years old singing "Don't worry about a thing" from the Bob Marley song, "Three Little Birds." The little guy was *feeling* that music, and his not worrying helped the listener not to worry too. This verse, the very living, breathing word of God, should make us feel this. And we should feel it on a deeper level than just listening to some reggae song, no matter *how* amazing it is.

Psalm 37 isn't the only "be still" found in the Bible that I want us to explore. One that is closely associated with the idea of rest is found in Psalm 46:10. It says, "Be still, and know that I am God; I will be exalted among the nations, I will be exalted in the earth."

The Hebrew word for "be still" used in this verse is the word *raphah* (pronounced raw-faw) and it means to sink or relax.[86] The word picture is of God is fighting for us so we can cease struggling. He is in control. I suggest reading this psalm in its entirety whenever you need a reminder that God is indeed *for* you. He is your refuge and strength and fortress. His presence is a place where you can stop the world and get off because you can sink into his grace and be safe from the chaos of life.

To continue to deepen our knowledge of what it means to be still, let's look at a story found in Exodus 14. The Hebrew people had just escaped Egypt. They had stopped at a place called Succoth, and the Lord had just told them to go to Pi Hahiroth. This pattern of travel made it look like they were aimlessly wandering in the desert. Pharaoh, who was hot and bothered that he'd let free labor slip out from under him, thought God's people were stupid and lost. He decided to pursue his former slaves—and not just with a few guys.

Pharaoh took six hundred of his best chariots, along with all the other fighting chariots in the whole country and headed out. From the best to the worst, if they had wheels, they were coming after God's people. The text tells us Pharaoh took *all* the chariots, *all* the horsemen, *all* the fighting horses, *all* the troops, and pursued his former slaves.

Basically, when the Hebrew people realized the entire force of Egypt was after them, they *lost* it. I guess if I had all that chasing me, I'd freak out too. The following verses in Exodus tells us the people were terrified. They cried out to the Lord and then to Moses, asking why they were in the desert in the first place. They were whining how they would have been better off living as slaves than dying in the desert.

Moses's response had to have been shocking to them. After all, he was getting chased down too! Here it is in Exodus 14:13–14:

> Moses answered the people, "Do not be afraid. Stand firm and you will see the deliverance the Lord will bring you today. The Egyptians you see today you will never see again. The Lord will fight for you; you need only to be still."

The first thing Moses told them was how to *feel*. So many times, we can't be still because of how we feel about a situation. The Bible tells us we are to take every thought captive, and that includes ponderings that are flooded with emotion. After he addressed their feelings, he hit them with a fact. You are going to see the Lord deliver you. And then Moses finishes strong with this doozy: "The Lord will fight for you; you need only to be still."

The Hebrew used for "be still" is a form of *charash*. It's a verb that means to cut in, to engrave, to plow, or to devise.[87] The idea is a word picture of scratching a line in the soil.[88] The translations of this picture are varied in our bibles—be calm, be silent, be still, be quiet, hold your peace. Couple this with earlier in the sentence when he told people to stand firm (Hebrew *yatsab*, to take a stand),[89] and we see Moses is telling the people to draw a line in the sand and pick their side.

The Israelites needed to dig their heels in and watch God move.

Have you ever felt threatened by something or someone, but you knew if you stopped and focused on the Lord, you'd see him take care of the situation? I once was in New Orleans with a group of students, and we were passing out water and food to homeless people close to St. Louis Cathedral. If you've been to Café Du Monde (and I hope you have), you were in the vicinity.

My group had been walking on the waterfront and had several great conversations and prayer with some homeless people after giving them food. We walked into a more populated area and ran into a witch doctor. Like a legit, scary, totally-possessed-but-not-by-Jesus kind of guy. By the time I realized who he was, it was too late. A conversation was going to happen.

I'll spare you the details, but after disagreeing with us and telling us we could pray *to him*, I decided to pray to the Real, One True God *in front* of him. Yes, my eyes were down, but they were wide open. I was completely aware we were in the presence of evil. The students felt it; I felt it. You could almost *see it* in his countenance.

Once we left, I knew we needed to debrief. It had been a crazy experience, and the students were shaky. We walked a bit and talked a second, and then stopped by a bench to break down the experience even more. A homeless man came up to us, and the conversation went something like this:

US: (Stopping the debrief...) Hey man, what's your name?
HIM: My name is Michael, like the angel.
US: Oh, cool. (Hunting for something else to say...) He was a messenger angel, right?
HIM: No. He is a warrior angel who fights for God's people.
US: (silence)
HIM: Let me read you some Scripture verses...

The students huddled around Michael as he read God's Word to them. Honestly, I didn't hear a thing. All I could think was how God had been fighting for us in that conversation with the witch doctor. All I could do was pray in silent praise and be in awe of our very personal God. Michael reminded me that God of the Universe was with us the entire time, taking care of us.

The Lord had fought for us; we just needed to be still.

Let's consider one other "be still" from the Bible; it is perhaps the most famous. It's in the New Testament where we find Jesus in a boat catching some z's. The book of Mark tells us there were other boats around them; tuck that away because that information is important for us later on. The weather had taken a horrible turn, and Mark says a "furious squall" came out of nowhere. The waves were coming over the side of the boat so forcefully that the disciples thought the boat was going to sink. They woke Jesus from his first-century waterbed and not very calmly cried, "Don't you care if we drown?" Jesus, as you know, got up and, in three simple words, rebuked the wind and the waves.

"Quiet! Be still!"

Can't you just see Jesus's response to his disciples? He didn't roll over with a grunt. He didn't tell them they'd be fine and let the storm rage around them. He responded by getting up and meeting them where they were. He answered their fears, and instead of muzzling their mouths, he muzzled the waves. Do you know that is the meaning of the Greek word used for "be still"? *Phimoo* means to muzzle or put to silence.[90]

When Jesus says be still, he means it. We need to remember he can calm the storm in any of us, offering rest. When we dig into our faith, we can swim in the silence of his grace. He offers a stillness like no other, and it is only found in and through a relationship with him. I hope you are living in his rest, and if not, why don't you stop and pray for it now.

In closing, remember those other boats on the lake with the disciples and Jesus? Who in your life is in a different boat—maybe a different type of life storm or situation than you—but they need the stillness of knowing God is in control around them? Stop and pray for them. Ask the Lord to bring a stillness to their hearts that can only come from the peace and completeness the Lord gives.

As for you—enjoy the ride. Jesus is with you in the boat. Whether the storm is raging or calm in your world right now, you need only to be still.

Chapter Questions

What are the various meanings of "Be Still"?

Which one means the most to you, and why?

Chapter Twenty-Seven

JUSTIFICATION AND HOPE

My husband is one of those people who can fix anything. He's built a motorcycle from the ground up, and we've saved more money on fixing cars than I can count. The first time I experienced his gift, we were dating and visiting his parents' house. I was inside talking with his mom, and Cory was hooking something audial into my car. He mentioned at one point that he might have to guide some wires under the hood, but that process wouldn't be too invasive. Knowing he understood cars, I didn't think twice about it. After twenty minutes of conversing with his mom, we both wondered what was taking so long.

I opened the back door and saw that everything that *should've* been under the hood was now *lying on the garage floor*. My expression must have been priceless because he laughed at my perfect timing and told me not to worry. He'd dropped a screw and had taken all the parts out, but he assured me he could put it back together, no problem. I just turned around and went back inside without a word. Cory does know cars inside and out; he did indeed have it up and running in no time. He knows cars because he understands each individual aspect of it. He has taken every part out, inspected it individually, and put each back only after he understands it. That's what I want us to do with this passage today. We are going to break it down, understand each major word, and then piece it back together with a deeper knowledge of what Paul was saying to us.

The first time I had to exegete, or take apart to understand, a passage of Scripture, I was a senior in college. I don't remember the name of the class, but I do remember the verses I chose: Romans 5:1–5. It was such a joy to break down what Paul was saying and understand it piece by piece. That is what we are going to do the next two chapters, and with the very same verses. Read the first part of it below.

Romans 5:1–2 says: "Therefore, since we have been justified through faith, we have peace with God through our Lord Jesus Christ, through whom we have gained access by faith into this grace in which we now stand. And we boast in the hope of the glory of God."

The first bolded word you read is "justified." I feel like this is a word we read a lot in Scripture. The Greek word here is *dikaioó*, and its meaning is simply *to be cleared of all charges*. It comes from the root word *dike*, which means to acquit.[91] To be justified is to be placed by God into a right relationship with himself.[92]

In the sentences below, we are going to replace some of the "church words" with their more everyday worded definitions. We are breaking down Scripture to words that are more easily understood so it can go into our brains, minds, and souls a little easier. Personally, if I don't stop and translate church words to where I understand them, I can miss the meaning of the passage. Instead of reading the word *justified*, let's replace it with "to be cleared of all charges."

Therefore, since we have been <u>cleared of all charges</u>...

It's already easier to understand what Paul is saying, isn't it?

Okay, so cleared of all charges through what? Next is the phrase *through faith*, which we covered in chapter nineteen. Remember how Moses's hands held steady until sunset? The definition of faith is being steadfast, firm, persistent, and sure.

Knowing that, I'm going add that to what I understand Romans 5:1 to say and read it like this: *Therefore, since we have been cleared of all charges <u>through being steadfast in the Lord</u>...*

To be clear, we are not changing Scripture or its meaning. We are breaking it down so we can understand it easier and on a deeper level, and so we can be equipped to share with others who may or may not be used to all our religious terminology.

Now that you see what I'm talking about, I'm going to let you into my head. This is how I read Romans 5:1... *Therefore, since we have been <u>cleared of all charges</u> through being steadfast in the Lord, we have <u>complete wholeness</u> with God through our Lord Jesus Christ, through whom we have gained access by <u>standing firm</u> in <u>his kind, unearned favor</u> in which we now stand...*

Does that make it easier for you to take to heart? It sure does for me. Now, let's move on to the next bolded word: *hope*. This is a word we really need to grasp, so we are going to hollow this one out, kind of like Cory did with my car. We then will return to Romans and finish the exegesis.

The Old Testament says blessed is the man whose hope is the Lord (Jeremiah 17:7 [KJV]). Romans 12:12 tells us we are to be joyful in hope and that Scriptures give us hope (Romans 15:4). Titus 2:13 reveals to us that Jesus is our blessed hope. All of that sounds important, so... what *is* hope? The Greek word is *elpis*, and means what hope means today—an expectation, anticipation, a trust, or a confidence.[93] The *Holman Bible Dictionary* takes it further and says it is a *trustful* expectation referencing the fulfillment of God's promises.[94] That is a wonderful, bright, beautiful thing. But the Hebraic concept of hope comes from a different angle and gives us a physical example to help us understand.

A few Hebraic words can be used for hope, but we are going to focus on the word *tiqvah*. It is found in Jeremiah 29:11, when it says God is going to give us hope and a future. Tiqvah is translated as hope, but *Strong's Concordance* says the meaning can also be "a cord." It comes from the related word *qavah*, which means an attachment or waiting in expectation. It can also mean to bind.[95]

The first time tiqvah is used in the Old Testament, we get to meet Rahab, who happened to be a prostitute. It's in the book of Joshua. When Joshua uses the word tiqvah, he is talking about a physical, scarlet cord. If you aren't familiar with the story, it takes place right after the death of Moses when the Israelites are about to enter the promised land.

Joshua is now in charge, and he sends two spies to check out the land, specifically the city of Jericho, where Rahab lives. As a great cover, these two spies spend the night with Rahab, the prostitute. The king of Jericho hears about the men, and folks around town somehow figured out these guys were not as innocent as they first seemed. The king asks Rahab to turn the men over to him. Instead, she covers for her new friends and says they've left town. She even sends the king's men on a wild goose chase to buy them some time.

Meanwhile, Rahab goes to the spies with an agreement. She and everyone else has heard about how the God of the Israelites was taking out anyone who opposed them. She made the men swear to be kind to her and her family since she had been kind to them, and she helped them escape through a window of her house that was a part of the city wall. To seal the deal, they handed her a scarlet tiqvah to put in her window. They told her that anyone inside the house with the red cord would be safe, but they were not to be held accountable for any family members not protected by the cord.

That cord tied Rahab to hope in a literal and figurative sense. It offered hope because that cord was physically the only thing keeping Rahab and her family safe. Without that cord, which bound them to the spy's vow of freedom and safety for Rahab and her family, they would die. But that cord was also symbolic because she had to wait and see if the spies would honor their agreement. In Rahab's hope of salvation, there was an expectation, a hope that something would happen.

The cord represented freedom and a future for Rahab. I wonder if she looked forward to not hitting the streets to make a living anymore. For her, only time would tell if her expectation was legitimate. For us, we have the answer. It's all the way in the New Testament.

Rahab is in the genealogy of Jesus.

Rahab's hope was in Israel. Jesus, our hope of salvation, came through her lineage. First Peter 1:3 says, "Praise be to the God and Father of our Lord Jesus Christ! In his great mercy he has given us new birth into a living hope through the resurrection of Jesus Christ from the dead…" Our hope should be tied to our Savior who has defeated sin and death and is alive today to anchor our very souls. Our hope isn't in a created thing or person but in the One who was and is and is to come!

Now that we understand hope on a deeper level, let's go back to Romans 5:2 where it says, "and we boast in the hope of the glory of God." Before we take the churchy words out, let's link it to the next thought. That hope, that cord, is connected to glory. Notice that hope can never stand alone. It has to be attached to something. That is why a Christian's hope is always found in Christ. So that verse in my mind would be read like this:

And we boast in the expectation and connection we have in the weight, honor, and importance of God.

It's a pretty earth-shattering thought that our hope and expectation is found in the glory and importance of God. Who we are, why we are on this earth, what our life is all about is only found in who God made us to be.

Now that we've translated church words into everyday language while keeping the meaning intact, ask the Lord to show you who in your life could use this joy and message of hope. And now, you can tell them about it in normal, everyday words over a cup of coffee!

Chapter Questions

What are the two definitions of hope?

How do both work together to give a fuller view of what it means to hope in Christ?

Chapter Twenty-Eight

SUFFERING, PERSEVERANCE, CHARACTER, AND HOPE

I grew up going to Opryland in Nashville, Tennessee. It was an amusement park with shows, roller coasters, huge swings, and the best log flume ever made. I vividly remember the soaked clothing sticking to my skin, the pungent aroma of fried funnel cakes, lots of laughter and fun, and those feelings of adventure only a twelve-year-old can have.

The roller coaster to casually weave into any prepubescent conversation was the Wabash Cannonball. I don't know how old I was when I first braved the mighty track, but I *do* remember I rode it eight times that first day. It offered everything I thought a coaster should have—ups, downs, sideways, and even a curly cue. As a kid, rides like that play on your emotions. As an adult, emotional roller coasters are no fun.

Some rides are a blast, like graduations, engagements, weddings, and babies. Others are painful, like dementia, cancer, divorce, and death. Because we are a communal people, we celebrate or grieve with one another again and again. I have experienced days where I joyfully celebrated a new baby and fifteen minutes later deeply mourned with someone over the loss of a loved one. Life is a journey of emotions and circumstances, but the Lord can always be found somewhere in each one.

Romans 5:1–5 encapsulates our spiritual journey in five short verses. It begins with being justified through faith in Christ and then walks through some cycles of life: suffering, perseverance, developing Christian character, and ending with hope. These stages aren't ridden just once but over and over to help us grow and mature in Christ.

In the last chapter, we really broke down Romans 5:1–2, and now we are going to tag on the remaining three verses. The words we are focusing on are fairly common. However, I do think it is important that we look closer to get a deeper understanding of each main word so we can see a clearer picture of this Scripture. Romans 5:3–5 says this,

> Not only so, but we also glory in our sufferings, because we know that suffering produces perseverance; perseverance, character; and character, hope. And hope does not put us to shame, because God's love has been poured out into our hearts through the Holy Spirit, who has been given to us.

Verse 3: We rejoice/glory in our sufferings...

This is a tough one, isn't it? Rejoicing in our suffering can be difficult to talk about and even harder to execute. Tim Keller said it well: "While other worldviews lead us to sit in the midst of life's joys, foreseeing the coming sorrows, Christianity empowers its people to sit in the midst of this world's sorrows, tasting the coming joy.[96] And that thought is exactly where this Scripture is taking us today.

By acknowledging suffering, we are giving weight to the pain we are dealing with.

The Greek word used in Romans 5:3 for suffering is *thlipsis* and conveys the idea of something that constricts or rubs together. It is describing a narrow place that hems someone in. It's talking about an internal pressure that causes one to feel restricted.[97] It also can be translated as persecution, affliction, distress, tribulation.[98] In short, easy language, suffering is pain.

If we are trying to live a life worthy of Christ, we are going to experience suffering. In America, we are blessed that any discomfort we may experience for the gospel is on a small, probably social scale. In other places in the world, the suffering is brutal. We, as believers, are to think different, act different; we *are* different. In certain cultures, Christianity means torture or death.

First Peter 5:10 reads, "And the God of all grace, who called you to his eternal glory in Christ, after you have suffered a little while, will himself restore you and make you strong, firm and steadfast."

Peter calls God the God of all grace. The God of kind, unearned favor. The God who has called us to a weighty life in Jesus Christ. Peter says this God, after we have suffered, will restore us. Sometimes this means in life. Sometimes this means in death. Suffering, no matter if large or small, is worth it. It is not in vain. Because when you read this verse, it doesn't say only some will suffer. Suffering is assumed on some level for all.

Did you catch the four things God promises after suffering for him?

1. Restoration
2. Strength
3. Firmness
4. Steadfastness

See those last two words? Those are two meanings of the Hebrew word *emunah* that is translated as faith. Suffering for the gospel increases our faith. It strengthens and restores us to be closer to whom he made us to be in Christ. This is one way that suffering produces perseverance, which takes us back to our Romans passage.

Suffering produces perseverance...

The Greek word for perseverance used here is *hupomoné* and means patient endurance or steadfastness.[99] Hupomoné comes from two words—*hypo*, meaning under, and *ménō*, meaning to remain or endure. The idea is remaining under something, like a challenge in life.[100]

What do perseverance and hope have in common? Perseverance is remaining in a challenge, and hope is waiting in expectation that good is going to come. They go hand in hand and build on each other. Perseverance without hope would be difficult. Hope without Jesus is impossible.

It is estimated that there are 400,000 Christians living in North Korea. Do you know how dangerous it is to become a Christian there? In that culture, the people know what happens to a person if he or she is "caught" following Jesus.

It is a death sentence.

Christians, when found out, will either be killed instantly or sent to a labor camp—both the Christian *and* his or her entire family, whether they are believers or not. These torturous death camps have inhumane conditions, and very few people make it out alive. It is estimated that 50,000 to 70,000 Christians are currently held in labor camps simply because of what they believe.[101] Yet... people are still coming to know Jesus. Even in this extreme suffering, North Korean believers are persevering for the Lord.

And perseverance, character...

Remember how the word *justified* comes from the Greek *dikaioo*? The Greek word for character is linked in meaning, and you see it in its spelling of *dokimé*. It means proof of genuineness, tested and true. Dokimé is tried, approved character.[102]

Perseverance lends itself to building character by being rooted and grounded in faith. My friend Eva knows this firsthand. Eva, a teenager at the time, was driving home from her boyfriend's house one cold evening. The roads were slick with ice, and she was on a tight two-lane country road. As she rounded a bend, a car was in her lane that had been trying to pass other vehicles and was coming at her, head on. Eva slammed on the breaks, missed the oncoming car, but hit an ice patch and lost control. She was headed straight for a bridge. She pumped the brakes again and began to spin. Her car flipped over a guardrail, rolled down a steep embankment, and ended up in a creek.

Eva's world changed that day. Her spinal cord had been severed in that accident. She was never going to be able to walk again. Instead of doing all the activities that go along with a senior year, Eva was in the hospital for the next several months. They had to rotate her bed so she wouldn't get pressure sores, and she spent hours staring, not at prom magazines and graduation invitations, but at the tiled hospital floor.

But Eva *persevered*.

It was a grueling task to learn things again. How to get dressed. Shower. Transfer from her wheelchair to another chair, a car, or the bed. She fought depression, anger, resentment, and hopelessness. Eva relied on the Lord every step of the way.

And God was faithful.

She was the first person in her family to attend college. There, she got involved with Fellowship of Christian Athletes and began to speak at various events. She spoke at churches, on the radio, and then was on stage in front of thousands at a time. Everywhere she went, Eva gave glory to the Lord. Eva met a great guy and got married. They have two beautiful fully-grown children.

Eva exudes joy and strength. The Lord built Eva's character in ways so deep and beautiful, you can't help but love her. He moves in her life in big and small ways all the time. Eva has gone through horrific trauma, yet she has love, peace, and hope. Like a diamond formed under pressure, Eva's life sparkles for Christ. She has found her purpose and hope in the Lord. She shares her story in her book, *May Bell's Daughter*.

And character, hope...

Romans 5:5 assures us that hope does not put us to shame. Isn't that beautiful? We started out this chapter with rejoicing in suffering. That seems like an oxymoron until we see that the entire process has constant underpinnings of hope. When we submit to the Lord in hard times, he offers hope. When we go at it alone, we have none.

Romans 5:1–5 is such a strong passage that summarizes the rhythm of life of one who is seeking the Lord. It's why we took two chapters to cover it! No matter what we are facing, when we submit to the Lord daily, we always have hope. When was the last time you stopped and thanked God for the hope he offers? If it's been a while, give it a go right now. If you are in a trial, ask him to help you persevere and teach you what you need to grow in your Christian character. And as you go about your day, rest in Hebrews 10:23, "Let us hold unswervingly to the hope we profess, for he who promised is faithful."

Chapter Question

Think about how these four concepts build on one another to bring hope. If one was left out, would the process be as effective?

Chapter Twenty-Nine

PREPARING, NOT CONFORMING, AND HAVING SELF-CONTROL

T he way my mom tells it, I started planning my own birthday parties when I was five. I loved the creativity, the festiveness, the decor, the games, the food—all of it. Planning the party was just as much fun as the actual day. Once I had my own children, my party planning reached epic proportions. We had ladybug parties, butterfly parties, and rock star parties. There have been superhero parties, tractor parties, and space parties.

My son's eighth birthday party was pirate themed. Everyone received eye patches and bandanas, and the party was all about the search for treasure. It was a scavenger hunt that ended literally with a bang: a piñata in the shape of a treasure chest. As a mom, it brought me great joy to watch the kids excitedly find pieces of the map and work together to figure out where the clue pointed them next. They were curious, engaged, and totally into the challenge.

My desire for you is to approach Scripture like a map of sorts, with curiosity and excitement. That brings joy to our Father in heaven. The word of God holds treasure for our souls, and when we let it define us, it is thrilling. So, let's dive into another great passage that defines how we should live and pick out each treasure piece by piece. First Peter 1:13–16 (ESV) says,

> Therefore, preparing your minds for action, and being sober-minded, set your hope fully on the grace that will be brought to you at the revelation of Jesus Christ. As obedient children, do not be conformed to the passions of your former ignorance, but as he who called you is holy, you also be holy in all your conduct, since it is written, "You shall be holy, for I am holy."

Prepare our minds for action...

The first piece of treasure we are going to examine is when Peter tells us our minds should be alert, focused on the expectancy of God's unearned kindness in our lives. If we are going to be defined by the Lord, understanding this verse is key! We should strive for this prepared mindset on a daily basis. So, how do we do that?

I want to encourage you to start each day with the Lord. In my quiet time, I read the Bible and talk to God in prayer. Some folks journal. I can tell you, if I miss my morning time with the Lord, I feel scattered, unsure, and a bit unsettled for the rest of the day. It's harder to control my thoughts, my actions, and my life. Preparing my mind for action really makes a difference for me, and I hope it does for you, too.

The Greek in 1 Peter 1:13 doesn't actually say "prepare our minds for action." Instead, it uses a common metaphor used in the culture of the day. It literally says, "having girded up the loins" of your mind... Isn't that great? The word used for this phrase is *anazonnumi,* and it means to gird or brace up. To gird up the loins meant tucking the bottom of the tunic into a belt so a person could work or run effectively. Peter was telling the readers to be prepared to move quickly wherever they needed to go and to arrive without delay in the Lord's will for that given day. He basically is saying, hey—be ready for God to move in and through your life!

And being sober minded...

You can see how Peter builds on this idea of readiness when he says to be sober-minded. He is telling us to be free from the influences of sin that can intoxicate us. I mean, really, does anyone make good decisions when intoxicated? Of course not. The very word intoxicated has the word toxic in the middle of it! Sin is toxic for our souls. It clouds our judgment, we lose control, and emotions can go out the window. In contrast, being sober-minded means a person has clear judgment, is under his or her own self-control, and temperate in nature.[103]

Set your hope fully on the grace that will be brought to you at the revelation of Jesus Christ...

After Peter has told us to be prepared, focused, and non-toxic, he starts talking about hope. Both definitions of hope can be seen here as it pertains to grace. Hope is living in the expectation of grace, as well as tying a cord that connects us to the unmerited favor of God. How amazing is that? But Peter doesn't stop and rest in hope. He keeps going!

As obedient children, do not be conformed to the passions of your former ignorance...

As God's children who listen to him and do what he says, we are to avoid conforming to the evil desires like one would who does not know the Lord. The word *conform* here in Greek is the verb *suschematizo* and means to fashion yourself after, to identify with, or to assume a similar outward form of something.[104] Basically, it means to imitate something. In other words, *don't imitate those who don't know Jesus.* This is the same word used in Romans 12:2 when it says do not be conformed to this world.

How many times do we as Christians fashion ourselves after the world in our speech, our mannerisms, our sarcasm, and our habits of what we let into our eyes, ears, and hearts? It is easy to avoid the large ways we should not conform—drunkenness, foul language, infidelity to spouse, and so forth—but we need to be aware of the smaller slopes on which we can slide. Are there any danger zone areas you need to keep in the forefront of your mind so you don't mimic the world? Each of us probably has a different struggle, but we all struggle with not conforming to *something.*

Our desire should be like David's in Psalm 19:14 when he says, "May these words of my mouth and this meditation of my heart be pleasing in your sight, Lord, my Rock and my Redeemer." You can even pray this psalm now as you focus your mind on the Lord if you'd like. Ask God to help your words, thoughts, and actions ultimately bring him glory. It is by daily yielding to his power that we continue to be transformed and become more Christlike.

But as he who called you is holy, you also be holy in all your conduct, since it is written, "You shall be holy, for I am holy..."

First Peter 1:15 tells us to be holy just as the Lord is holy. We can set ourselves apart from worldly things, but we can only be classified as holy when we participate in the holiness the Lord has given us. It is through being tuned in to the Holy Spirit that we can be refined and see things from a spiritual point of view rather than a physical one.

Remember, holiness can be defined as above and beyond, yet choosing to reach in and interact with something or someone. From the beginning to end of this 1 Peter passage, we have honed in on being prepared, having self-control, setting our minds on hope, and experiencing grace.

We have been reminded of the importance of obedience to God rather than conforming to the world. And ultimately, after we have done these things, we end up being a reflection and a vessel of God's holiness. Isn't God's holiness where this whole book began?

Chapter Question

Why is it so important that we prepare our minds for action?

Chapter Thirty

REMEMBER

hope you have enjoyed defining biblical words in their original languages and that you feel more empowered to share God's Word with those around you. My prayer is that this book has broadened your understanding of the Scriptures, deepened your faith, and that you have engaged with God's Word to the point you are actively incorporating this new knowledge into your life when you sing worship songs, read Scripture, and even when you pray. My goal for you after this study is that you *remember* what you have learned.

Remember.

To us, that word means thinking about something we've previously done or experienced in thought, conversation, or learning environment. It's simply bringing something to the forefront of our mind. But in biblical culture, it is much more complex than a memory pattern of your brain.

The Hebrew word for remember is *zakhar*, and its definition joins together the thought of remembering with the actions that result from those memories.[105] Biblical Hebraic verbs simply don't stay confined to a thought. Instead, they promote an action done out of an idea. The first time we see this in Scripture is Genesis 8:1, when it says God *remembered* Noah.

Wait, does this mean God *forgot* about Noah?

Of course not. God never wondered who the guy was in the boat with all the weird pets. The Hebrew verb of remembering focuses on the action of what God was doing, not his memory. The following verses proceed to tell us exactly what God did after he "remembered" Noah. The flood waters began to recede, and eventually dry land was seen again. The Bible contains other examples of when God remembered. He remembered Rachel (Genesis 30:22) and Hannah (1 Samuel 1:19) and gave them children. He remembered Abraham by keeping his nephew Lot safe. When God remembers someone in the Bible, it is always accompanied by an action.

Can you think of some ways God has remembered you?

Psalm 105:1–8 talks about remembering and gives some great tips on how we can "remember" the Lord in our lives.

Give praise to the Lord, proclaim his name; make known among the nations what he has done. Sing to him, sing praise to him; tell of all his wonderful acts. Glory in his holy name; let the hearts of those who seek the Lord rejoice. Look to the Lord and his strength; seek his face always. Remember the wonders he has done, his miracles, and the judgments he pronounced, you his servants, the descendants of Abraham, his chosen ones, the children of Jacob. He is the Lord our God; his judgments are in all the earth. He remembers his covenant forever, the promise he made, for a thousand generations...

These verses are packed full of ways we can remember God. In the first four verses alone, nine actions are listed to help us remember God.

1. Give praise to the Lord.
2. Proclaim his name.
3. Make known what he has done.
4. Sing praises to him.
5. Tell of his wonderful acts.
6. Glory in his name.
7. Rejoice as you seek him.
8. Look to the Lord's strength.
9. Seek him always.

But we aren't the only ones doing the remembering in this psalm. Verse 8 tells us that the Lord will *remember* his covenant with us forever.

Forever.

What a beautiful and awesome God we serve. Our God will never forget us; he will never leave us; he will never abandon us (Deuteronomy 31:6). His memory isn't something we have to fear in the negative sense of things. He is a God worthy or worship and honor and praise. He will always remember the new covenant he made with us in Jesus Christ (Hebrews 9:15), yet he will *not* remember our sin. Jeremiah 31:33–34 tells us,

"This is the covenant I will make with the people of Israel after that time," declares the Lord. "I will put my law in their minds and write it on their hearts. I will be their God, and they will be my people. No longer will they teach their neighbor, or say to one another, 'Know the Lord,' because they will all know me, from the least of them to the greatest," declares the Lord. "For I will forgive their wickedness and will remember their sins no more."

That's the best of both worlds, isn't it? We see forgiveness, grace, and mercy all wrapped up in how God chooses to remember—or not remember—in his relationship with us.

When we realize how all-encompassing the blessings of God are, we see through a clearer lens how God remembers us every day. Our God is a personal God, filled with compassion, healing, truth, and justice. The biblical meaning of remember encompasses all of this and so much more. I don't know about you, but it is incredibly humbling knowing that God is *for* me. My mind echoes Hebrews 2:6 (NLT): "What are mere mortals that you should think about them, human beings that you should care for them?" The God of the Universe remembers me with blessings. He does not remember or define me by my mistakes and sins that I have confessed and repented from. They are left in the past. Doesn't it make you in awe of our Holy God?

That awe brings us full circle in this book. We find ourselves staring into the face of holiness. Only a Holy God would treat his children this way. Only a God who is above and beyond, but chooses to reach down and interact, could have such an all-encompassing love for sinners saved by grace.

Now that we are familiar with the Hebrew definition of remember, we can no longer be content with simply thinking about God and call it remembering. When we remember God in our lives, we must act. We must forgive. Offer mercy. Be generous. Be thankful. Be kind. We must love God with our heart and soul and mind and strength—*not* just as a fleeting thought—and we must love our neighbors as ourselves. We must reach into the world to interact but be above and beyond the world when we love.

Looking back at 1 Peter 1:16, we see Peter is quoting Leviticus 11:45. It tells us that God commands us to be holy because he is holy. We must remember this is a command—not a suggestion, good idea, or option. When we remember the holiness of God, the result is a desire and mindset to become holy ourselves.

We must not forget the greatness of who defines us,
for he who defines us is too great himself to be defined.

Without the Lord, we will never be holy. But the power of the Holy Spirit is inside us, helping us remember who he is and equipping us to be more like him. Remembering the Lord's commands means applying them wholeheartedly to our lives every day. Look at what John 14:26 tells us about the role of the Holy Spirit in our lives: "But the Advocate, the Holy Spirit, whom the Father will send in my name, will teach you all things and will remind you of everything I have said to you."

Don't simply be reminded. Make it a point to remember. Remember what you have learned in this study. Remember by living out the Lord's commands. Remember joy, peace, grace, hope, humility, and wisdom. Remember by living a holy life that is filled with awe, forgiveness, and faithfulness.

Remember in confession and repentance. Remember by living in positive fear and reveling in the victory you have found in Christ. Remember that you are justified, redeemed, and restored. Remember that you are a child of the king.

Remember it is *he* who made you.
He who is for you.
And it is *he* who deeply defines you soul.

NEXT STEPS

A re you interested in becoming even more *Deeply Defined*? You can turn this book into a group study for your church!

We have **FREE Small Group Discussion Guides** available that transform *Deeply Defined* into a six-week Bible study, perfect for a small group! To download the discussion guides—or to see Janey's availability to speak at your church, retreat, or event—go to **www.JaneyPitts.com.**

And… if you enjoyed this book, please share it with others! Take a selfie with your *Deeply Defined* book wherever you are—at the beach, camping, in your favorite chair, or visiting an exciting place! Then put it on Instagram or Facebook with a review of why your friends should read it, and hashtag your post with **#DeeplyDefined.** We will feature many of them and share on our website and/or social media pages!

Social Media
If you'd like to connect with Janey, follow her on these platforms…

- **Facebook:** https://www.facebook.com/OfficialJaneyPitts
- **Instagram:** https://www.instagram.com/OfficialJaneyPitts
- **Website:** https://www.JaneyPitts.com

Extra Resources for You

In the next few pages, you will find a list of all the defined words from this study. Please use it as a reference in your personal time with the Lord. It is designed to be a resource to help you remember the meanings of words directly from the culture of the Bible and the original languages in which it was written. Use it, share it with others, make notes in your bible. It is there to help you grow ever deeper into God's Word!

DEFINITIONS

amen. Confirm or support, to be in agreement with.

believe. Confirm or support, firm.

be still.
   damam (Hebrew). Rest, to be or to grow silent or still
   raphah (Hebrew). To sink or relax, cease fighting.
   charash (Hebrew). To cut in engrave, to plow, to devise; to "dig deep in your faith."
   phimoo (Greek). To muzzle or put to silence.

character. Proof of genuineness; tested and true. Dokime is tried, approved character.

confess. To voice the same conclusion, to be in full agreement with, to acknowledge, to admit.

conform. To fashion yourself after, to identify with, or assume a similar outward form of something.

contrite. Crushed or pulverized like powder.

faith/faithful.
   emunah (Hebrew). Firmness, steadfast, fidelity, persistent, sure.
   pistis (Greek). Faith, trust, believe.

fear.
   phobos (Greek). To fear, withdraw, flee, or avoid.
   yirat (Hebrew). To be afraid, to draw away from; to revere or drawn toward in awe.

foolish. Wear away, crumble, wither, fall and fade; to be senseless, to treat with contempt.

forgiveness. A restorative relationship that entails the removal of guilt.
   nasa (Hebrew). To lift, carry, or forgive.
   kaphar (Hebrew). To cover or atone for sin.
   salach (Hebrew). To pardon or forgive.
   aphiemi (Greek). To send away from, leave alone, permit to depart; suffer.

fret (Hebrew root charas). To burn or to be kindled with anger.

glory. Originally battle armaments; heavy, weighty; of importance; gives or shows honor.

good. Something pleasant or agreeable; something that functions properly.

gospel. VICTORY; the good news of freedom we find in Jesus's death, burial, and resurrection.
   bisar (Hebrew).
   euangelion (Greek).

grace. I love you anyway.
   chen (Hebrew, from chanan). To bend down to; kindness from a superior to an inferior. Steadfast love, unmerited favor.
   charis (Greek). That which affords joy, pleasure, delight, sweetness, and charm.

hear. To obey.

holiness. Set apart; measureless; above and beyond; yet chooses to reach into our world and interact.

hope. Can mean or is related to a cord, an expectation, an attachment, or waiting on something.

humility. A personal quality where someone shows dependence on God and respect for others.

idol.
   Atsabh, Etseb, and Otseb (Hebrew). A cause of grief.

joy. Inner gladness, delight; happiness caused by a spiritual reality rather than human circumstance; a fruit of the spirit.

justified. To be cleared of all charges; from root word meaning to acquit.

iniquity. A premeditated sin that continues in a person's life without remorse or repentance.

mercy. Mercy is undeserved favor shown out of compassion from a superior to an inferior, with an element of withholding what is deserved; compassion or forgiveness shown toward someone whom it is within one's power to punish or harm; mercy, compassion, active pity, with the sense of goodness in general, especially piety.

obey. To hear and do.

overcome. To conquer, prevail; to carry off the victory, come off victorious.

peace. Complete, whole; to restore or make right through restitution.

perseverance. Endurance; remaining under; steadfastness.

prepare. To gird or brace up. It was a metaphor of tucking the bottom of the tunic into the top so one could work or run effectively. Peter was telling the readers to be prepared to move quickly wherever they needed to go and to arrive without delay.

redeem. To be set free by paying the full price; to restore something back into the possession of its rightful owner; rescue from the power of an alien possessor.

remember. The thought of remembering through actions that result from those memories, not just a memory with no action attached.

remain. Abide, to stay; to continue to be.

repent. Change of mind, purpose, or attitude.
  meta (Greek prefix). Movement or change.
  noeo (Greek suffix). Thoughts, perceptions, dispositions, purposes.
  teshuvah (Hebrew). To return.

righteousness. Living in the right according to God.

salvation.
  yasa (Hebrew). To rescue, to deliver, and to bring to safety; health, well-being and healing.
  soteria (Greek). Deliverance, salvation; welfare, prosperity, preservation, safety.
  sozo (Greek). Save or rescue.

self-control. "Sober-minded." Peter is telling us to be free from illusion, from the influences of sin that can intoxicate us. It's having clear judgment, being self-controlled, and temperate.

shekinah. That which dwells.

shema. To hear, to obey; hearing that brings obedience.

sin. To miss the mark, to do something in error.

suffering. The idea of something that constricts or rubs together, or of a narrow place that "hems someone in."

sufficient. Enough; equal to the end proposed.

supplication (also petition). Comes out of a place of deep need, a place of lacking.

transcend. To rise above, to be superior to.

transgression. A revolt, an active rebellion or defiance against an authority; willful deviation from the path of righteousness; *active rebellion or defiance against God.* Is same as trespass.

trespass. Active rebellion or defiance against God.

troubled. To agitate back and forth, to shake to and fro, or to set in motion that which is supposed to be still.

trust. To cling to something or someone; to find security.

wait patiently. To whirl, dance, or writhe in pain.

wicked. One guilty of a crime, one deserving punishment.

wisdom. Learned, cultivated, skilled, clever; judging correctly and following best course of action.

woe. A judgment or grief beyond description on someone or a group.

ABOUT THE AUTHOR

Janey graduated from Samford University and earned her Masters in Religious Education from Southwestern Baptist Theological Seminary. She has served on church staffs for over fifteen years and serves on the same staff with her husband, Cory, as the Missions Mobilizer at New Work Fellowship in Hopkinsville, Kentucky. Janey and Cory have two children together. She enjoys speaking at various events and retreats and would love to speak at yours. To book Janey for your event, check out her website at **www.JaneyPitts.com**.

ENDNOTES

Chapters 1-5

1   Pryor, Dwight A. "Holy! Holy! Holy!, Part One: The Dimensions of the Holy." MP3 audio, JC Studies, https://www.jcstudies.store/holy-holy-holy/.

2   Gess, Lowell A. Tender Moments in Ministry. Alexandria, MN: Dr. Lowell Gess, 2018.

3   Tozer, A. W. The Knowledge of the Holy. HarperOne, 2009.

4   Buratti, Bonnie, William B. Hubbard, and Mark Marley. "Saturn." Encyclopædia Britannica Inc. https://www.britannica.com/place/Saturn-planet.

5   Dunbar, Brian. "Ring-a-Round the Saturn." NASA, May 21, 2015. https://www.nasa.gov/audience/forstudents/k-4/stories/nasa-knows/ring-a-round-the-saturn.html.

6   Zodhiates, Spiros. The Complete Word Study Old Testament. Chattanooga: AMG Publishers, 2002.

7   "Shekinah Definition and Meaning—Bible Dictionary." Biblestudytools.com. https://www.biblestudytools.com/dictionary/shekinah/.

8 Spurgeon, C. H. The Treasury of David. Nashville, TN: Thomas Nelson, 1984.

9 Sproul, R. C. The Holiness of God. Tyndale House Publishers, 1998.

10 Pryor, Dwight A. "Holy! Holy! Holy!, Part One: The Dimensions of the Holy."

11 Luther, Martin. Epistles of St. Peter and St. Jude Preached and Explained. Trajectory, Inc. 2014.

12 Tozer, A. W. The Pursuit of God: The Human Thirst for the Divine. Chicago: Moody Publishers, 2015.

13 Zodhiates, Spiros. The Complete Word Study Old Testament.

14 Zodhiates, Spiros. The Complete Word Study Old Testament.

15 Zodhiates, Spiros. The Complete Word Study Old Testament.

16 Merriam-Webster.com Dictionary, s.v. "confession," https://www.merriam-webster.com/dictionary/confession

17 "Webster's Dictionary 1828—Repent." Webster's Dictionary 1828. http://webstersdictionary1828.com/Dictionary/repent.

Chapter 6–10

18 HELPS Word-studies: 3670. homologeó—to speak the same, to agree. https://biblehub.com/greek/3670.htm.

19 Owen, John. The Mortification of Sin. United States: CreateSpace, 2013.

20 Piper, John. What Jesus Demands from the World. Crossway Books, 2011.

21 Tverberg, Lois. "The Joy of Repentance." En-Gedi Resource Center, July 15, 2015. https://engediresourcecenter.com/2015/07/07/the-joy-of-repentance/.

22 Brown-Driver-Briggs: 7563. rasha—wicked, criminal. https://biblehub.com/hebrew/7563.htm.

23 "Forgiveness Definition and Meaning—Bible Dictionary." Biblestudy-tools.com. https://www.biblestudytools.com/dictionary/forgiveness/.

24 Strong's Concordance #5375: nasa—Greek/Hebrew Definitions—Bible Tools. https://www.bibletools.org/index.cfm/fuseaction/Lexicon.show/ID/H5375/nasa.htm.

25 Strong's Concordance #3722: kaphar—Greek/Hebrew Definitions—Bible Tools. https://www.bibletools.org/index.cfm/fuseaction/Lexicon.show/ID/H3722/kaphar.htm.

26 Strong's Concordance: 5545. salach—to forgive, pardon. https://biblehub.com/hebrew/5545.htm.

27 Strong's Concordance #863: aphiemi—Greek/Hebrew Definitions—Bible Tools. https://www.bibletools.org/index.cfm/fuseaction/Lexicon.show/ID/G863/aphiemi.htm.

28 Lewis, C. S. "On Forgiveness." The Weight of Glory: And Other Addresses. HarperOne, 2001.

Chapter 11–15

29 Zodhiates, Spiros. The Complete Word Study Old Testament..

30 Mills, Watson E., and Roger Aubrey Bullard. Mercer Dictionary of the Bible. Macon, GA: Mercer University Press, 1992.

31 "MERCY: Definition of MERCY by Oxford Dictionary on Lexico.com." Lexico Dictionaries | English. Lexico Dictionaries. https://www.lexico.com/en/definition/mercy.

32 Zodhiates, Spiros. The Complete Word Study Dictionary: New Testament. Chattanooga TN: AMG Publishers, 1992.

33 "David Dancing before the Ark Because of His Election." The Spurgeon Center, July 1, 1888. https://www.spurgeon.org/resource-library/sermons/david-dancing-before-the-ark-because-of-his-election/#flipbook/.

34 Strong's #2603: chanan—Greek/Hebrew Definitions—Bible Tools. https://www.bibletools.org/index.cfm/fuseaction/Lexicon.show/ID/ H2603/chanan.htm.

35 Douglas, James D., and Merrill C. Tenney. The New International Dictionary of the Bible. Grand Rapids, MI: Zondervan, 1987.

36 Jeremiah, David. Captured By Grace: No One Is Beyond the Reach of a Loving God. Nashville, TN: Thomas Nelson, 2010.

37 Strong's #5485: charis—Greek/Hebrew Definitions—Bible Tools. https://www.bibletools.org/index.cfm/fuseaction/Lexicon.show/ID/ G5485/charis.htm.

38 "Webster's Dictionary 1828—Sufficient." Webster's Dictionary 1828. http://webstersdictionary1828.com/Dictionary/sufficient.

39 Taunton Family Children's Home. https://www.tauntonhome.net/.

40 Strong's Concordance #5259: hupo—Greek/Hebrew Defini- tions—Bible Tools. https://www.bibletools.org/index.cfm/ fuseaction/Lexicon.show/ID/G5259/hupo.htm.

41 Bonhoeffer, Dietrich. The Cost of Discipleship. Touchstone, 2018.

42 HELPS Word-studies: 3084. lutroó—to release by paying a ransom, to redeem. https://biblehub.com/greek/3084.htm.

43 Bonhoeffer, Dietrich. The Cost of Discipleship.

44 Yancey, Philip. Vanishing Grace: Whatever Happened to the Good News. Grand Rapids, MI: Zondervan, 2014.

Chapter 16–20

45 Merriam-Webster.com Dictionary, s.v. "gospel," https://www. merriam-webster.com/dictionary/gospel.

46 Butler, Trent C. Holman Bible Dictionary. Nashville, TN: Holman Bible Publishers, 1991.

47 Butler, Trent C. Holman Bible Dictionary.

48 Butler, Trent C. Holman Bible Dictionary.

49 Butler, Trent C. Holman Bible Dictionary.

50 Strong's #3528: nikao—Greek/Hebrew Definitions—Bible Tools.
    https://www.bibletools.org/index.cfm/fuseaction/Lexicon.show/ID/
    G3528/nikao.htm

51 Strong's #3529: nike—Greek/Hebrew Definitions—Bible Tools.
    https://www.bibletools.org/index.cfm/fuseaction/Lexicon.show/ID/
    G3529/nike.htm.

52 Strong's Concordance #4991: soteria—Greek/Hebrew Defini-
    tions—Bible Tools. https://www.bibletools.org/index.cfm/fuseac-
    tion/Lexicon.show/ID/G4991/soteria.htm.

53 Strong's #4982: sozo—Greek/Hebrew Definitions—Bible Tools.
    https://www.bibletools.org/index.cfm/fuseaction/Lexicon.show/ID/
    G4982/sozo.htm.

54 Zodhiates, Spiros. The Complete Word Study Old Testament.

55 Wilson, Marvin R. Our Father Abraham: Jewish Roots of the
    Christian Faith. Eerdmans, 1990. (And let me just say that I have
    emailed Dr. Wilson several times with questions, and he is gracious,
    outstanding, and cool as grits. I'm a HUGE "Marv" fan.)

56 "Definition of Natzeret Meaning and Definition." BibliaTodo.
    https://www.bibliatodo.com/en/bible-dictionary/natzeret.

57 Elwell, Walter A. Evangelical Dictionary of Biblical Theology
    (Baker Reference Library). Grand Rapids: Baker Book House,
    1996.

58 Tverberg, Lois. Walking in the Dust of Rabbi Jesus. Grand Rapids,
    MI: Zondervan, 2011.

59 Tverberg, Lois. Walking in the Dust of Rabbi Jesus.

60 Strong's Concordance Greek: 191. akouo—to hear, listen. https://
    biblehub.com/greek/191.htm.

61 Mills, Watson E., and Roger Aubrey Bullard. Mercer Dictionary of
    the Bible. Macon, GA: Mercer University Press, 1992.

62 Mills, Watson E., and Roger Aubrey Bullard. Mercer Dictionary of
    the Bible.

63 "Hebrew Definitions." Precept Austin. https://www.preceptaustin.
org/hebrew_definitions.
64 Strong's Concordance Greek: 530. emunah—firmness, steadfastness, fidelity. https://biblehub.com/greek/530.htm.
65 Butler, Trent C. Holman Bible Dictionary.

Chapter 21–25

66 Cloud, Dr. Henry. Necessary Endings: The Employees, Businesses,
and Relationships That All of Us Have to Give Up in Order to
Move Forward. New York: HarperCollins, 2011.
67 Brown, Francis, S. R. Driver, and Charles A. Briggs. The Brown,
Driver, Briggs Hebrew and English Lexicon. Peabody, MA: Hen-
drickson Publishers, 2015.
68 Douglas, James D., and Merrill C. Tenney. The New International
Dictionary of the Bible. Grand Rapids, MI: Zondervan, 1987.
69 Strong's Concordance #5401: phobos—Greek/Hebrew Definitions—Bible Tools. https://www.bibletools.org/index.cfm/fuseac-
tion/Lexicon.show/ID/G5401/phobos.htm.
70 Douglas, James D., and Merrill C. Tenney. The New International
Dictionary of the Bible.
71 Butler, Trent C. Holman Bible Dictionary.
72 Strong's Concordance Greek: 1166. deiknumi—to show. https://
biblehub.com/greek/1166.htm.
73 Strong's Concordance #2896: towb—Greek/Hebrew Definitions—
Bible Tools. https://www.bibletools.org/index.cfm/fuseaction
/Lexicon.show/ID/H2896/towb.htm.
74 Benner, Jeff A. The Ancient Hebrew Lexicon of the Bible. College
Station, TX: Virtualbookworm.com Publishing, 2005.
75 Strong's Concordance #3306: meno — Greek/Hebrew Definitions
— Bible Tools. https://www.bibletools.org/index.cfm/fuseaction/
Lexicon.show/ID/G3306/meno.htm.

76   Merriam-Webster.com Dictionary, s.v. "remain," https://www. merriam-webster.com/dictionary/remain.

77   "Joy—Chara (Greek Word Study)." Precept Austin. https://www. preceptaustin.org/joy_-_chara.

78   Benner, Jeff A. The Ancient Hebrew Lexicon of the Bible.

79   Benner, Jeff A. The Ancient Hebrew Lexicon of the Bible.

80   Strong's Concordance #5015: tarasso—Greek/Hebrew Definitions—Bible Tools. https://www.bibletools.org/index.cfm/fuseaction/Lexicon.show/ID/G5015/tarasso.htm.

81   Strong's Concordance #1162: deesis—Greek/Hebrew Definitions—Bible Tools. https://www.bibletools.org/index.cfm/fuseaction/Lexicon.show/ID/G1162/deesis.htm.

82   Strong's Concordance Greek: 5242. huperechó—to hold above, to rise above, to be superior. https://biblehub.com/greek/5242.htm

83   Chapter 26–30
Strong's Concordance #1826: damam—Greek/Hebrew Definitions—Bible Tools. https://www.bibletools.org/index.cfm/fuseaction/Lexicon.show/ID/H1826/damam.htm.

84   Strong's Concordance #2342: chuwl—Greek/Hebrew Definitions—Bible Tools. https://www.bibletools.org/index.cfm/fuseaction/Lexicon.show/ID/H2342/chuwl.htm.

85   Benner, Jeff A. The Ancient Hebrew Lexicon of the Bible.

86   Strong's Concordance #7503: raphah—Greek/Hebrew Definitions—Bible Tools. https://www.bibletools.org/index.cfm/fuseaction/Lexicon.show/ID/H7503/raphah.htm.

87   Strong's Concordance #2790: charash—Greek/Hebrew Definitions—Bible Tools. https://www.bibletools.org/index.cfm/fuseaction/Lexicon.show/ID/H2790/charash.htm.

88   Benner, Jeff A. The Ancient Hebrew Lexicon of the Bible.

89   Strong's Concordance #3320: yatsab—Greek/Hebrew Defini-
     tions—Bible Tools. https://www.bibletools.org/index.cfm/
     fuseaction/Lexicon.show/ID/H3320/yatsab.htm.

90   Strong's Concordance #5392: phimoo—Greek/Hebrew Defini-
     tions—Bible Tools. https://www.bibletools.org/index.cfm/
     fuseaction/Lexicon.show/ID/G5392/phimoo.htm.

91   HELPS Word-studies: 1344. dikaioó—to show to be righteous,
     declare righteous. https://biblehub.com/greek/1344.htm.

92   Douglas, James D. and Merrill C. Tenney. The New International
     Dictionary of the Bible. Grand Rapids, MI: Zondervan, 1987.

93   Strong's Concordance #1680: elpis—Greek/Hebrew Definitions—
     Bible Tools. https://www.bibletools.org/index.cfm/fuseaction/
     Lexicon.show/ID/G1680/elpis.htm.

94   Butler, Trent C. Holman Bible Dictionary.

95   Strong's Concordance #8615: tiqvah—Greek/Hebrew Defini-
     tions—Bible Tools. https://www.bibletools.org/index.cfm/
     fuseaction/Lexicon.show/ID/H8615/tiqvah.htm.

96   Keller, Timothy. Walking with God Through Pain and Suffering.
     New York: Penguin Books, 2016.

97   HELPS Word-studies: 2347. thlipsis—tribulation. https://
     biblehub.com/greek/2347.htm.

98   Strong's Concordance #2347: thlipsis—Greek/Hebrew Defini-
     tions—Bible Tools. https://www.bibletools.org/index.cfm/
     fuseaction/Lexicon.show/ID/G2347/thlipsis.htm.

99   Strong's Concordance #5281: hupomoné—Greek/Hebrew Defini-
     tions—Bible Tools. https://www.bibletools.org/index.cfm/
     fuseaction/Lexicon.show/ID/G5281/hupomone.htm.

100 HELPS Word-studies: 5281. hypomoné—a remaining behind, a
    patient enduring. https://biblehub.com/greek/5281.htm.

101 "North Korea." Open Doors USA, January 13, 2021. https://www.opendoorsusa.org/christian-persecution/world-watch-list/north-korea/.

102 HELPS Word-studies: 1382. dokimé—(the process or result of) trial, proving, approval. https://biblehub.com/greek/1382.htm.

103 HELPS Word-studies: 3525. néphó—to be sober, to abstain from wine. https://biblehub.com/greek/3525.htm.

104 Strong's Concordance #4964: suschematizo—Greek/Hebrew Definitions—Bible Tools. https://www.bibletools.org/index.cfm/fuseaction/Lexicon.show/ID/G4964/suschematizo.htm

105 Brown, Francis, S. R. Driver, and Charles A. Briggs. The Brown, Driver, Briggs Hebrew and English Lexicon.

A free ebook edition is available with the purchase of this book.

To claim your free ebook edition:

1. Visit MorganJamesBOGO.com
2. Sign your name CLEARLY in the space
3. Complete the form and submit a photo of the entire copyright page
4. You or your friend can download the ebook to your preferred device

Morgan James BOGO™

A **FREE** ebook edition is available for you or a friend with the purchase of this print book.

_____

CLEARLY SIGN YOUR NAME ABOVE

Instructions to claim your free ebook edition:
1. Visit MorganJamesBOGO.com
2. Sign your name CLEARLY in the space above
3. Complete the form and submit a photo of this entire page
4. You or your friend can download the ebook to your preferred device

Print & Digital Together Forever.

Snap a photo

Free ebook

Read anywhere